MR

1 Da

A

D

D1140833

POMPEII

POMPEII
THE LAST DAY

Dr Paul Wilkinson

BBC BOOKS

Published to accompany the television programme
Pompeii, first broadcast on BBC 1 in 2003.
Producer: Ailsa Orr
Executive producer: Michael Mosley

First published 2003 © copyright Dr Paul Wilkinson
The moral right of the author has been asserted.

All rights reserved. No part of this book may be
reproduced in any form or by any means without prior written
permission from the publisher, except by a reviewer who may
quote brief passages in a review.

ISBN 0 563 48770 4

Published by BBC Books, BBC Worldwide Ltd,
Woodlands, 80 Wood Lane, London W12 0TT

Commissioning editor: Shirley Patton
Project editor: Helena Caldon
Copy-editor: Lee Johnson
Art director: Linda Blakemore
Designer: Bill Mason
Picture researcher: Deirdre O'Day
Production controller: Christopher Tinker

Set in Foundry Old Style
Printed and bound in Great Britain by
Butler & Tanner Ltd, Frome
Colour separations by Radstock Reproductions Ltd,
Midsomer Norton
Jacket printed by Lawrence-Allen Ltd,
Weston-super-Mare

CONTENTS

Chapter Four:
The Public Buildings
98

Chapter Five:
Private Homes
140

Chapter Six:
A Day's Guide to Pompeii
160

INTRODUCTION

The names of Pompeii and Herculaneum epitomise the lost glories of ancient Rome and their dramatic end is a poignant reminder of a great empire and culture. The ruins of these towns resonate so strongly with those living in the modern world that they are among the most popular destinations for travellers fascinated by Roman culture. Since the eighteenth century, the towns have attracted the scholar and tourist alike, with more than two million people each year visiting Pompeii alone.

Above This painting by Jacob Philipp Hacket (1737–1809) shows Pompeii as it would have looked to eighteenth-century visitors on the Grand Tour.

After the eruption of Mount Vesuvius, in AD 79, Pompeii and Herculaneum lay buried and forgotten by later generations for over 1,500 years. All that remained was the memory of the towns in ancient descriptions, and the occasional attempts of local antiquarians to identify the sites. The towns attracted little interest until the eighteenth century, when the ruins of both towns were discovered accidentally. Herculaneum was found beneath metres of solidified volcanic debris when a workman digging a well penetrated its theatre. But it was not the architecture that attracted attention, it was the statues and precious marble facings used by the Romans. The Austrian Prince d'Elbeuf was building a villa nearby, so, from 1709 to 1716, he removed the beautiful marbles and statues from the Roman theatre. He enlarged the well shaft and opened up tunnels to bring up the exquisite relics from this underground treasure trove. Once his villa was decorated, all investigations ceased for more than 20 years.

Pompeii was similarly discovered during construction work. In the sixteenth century an underground irrigation canal from the River Sarno cut through numerous buried Roman buildings whose walls were decorated with frescoes. An inscription was found of the word 'Pompeii' and the architect of the canal, Fortuna, thought he had stumbled on a villa belonging to Pompeius. He had, in fact, discovered the city of Pompeii.

Herculaneum and Pompeii remained buried until the mid-eighteenth century when the ruler of Naples, the future Charles III of Spain, ordered a systematic investigation of the Bay of Naples area. Although the finds were reported, the aim of the investigations was to recover precious objects to decorate the royal court. So the chance discovery and subsequent looting of the sites meant that few appreciated what they found. It would be some time before the buried tragedy of Herculaneum and Pompeii would be revealed.

THE FOUNDING OF POMPEII AND HERCULANEUM

Pompeii and Herculaneum were but two of several Roman towns along the coast of the Bay of Naples living under the shadow of an active volcano. The foundation of both towns pre-dates the Roman conquest of Campania, however. Herculaneum and Pompeii are thought to date back to the seventh century BC, with possibly some earlier settlement at Pompeii.

The towns and communities at both Pompeii and Herculaneum were

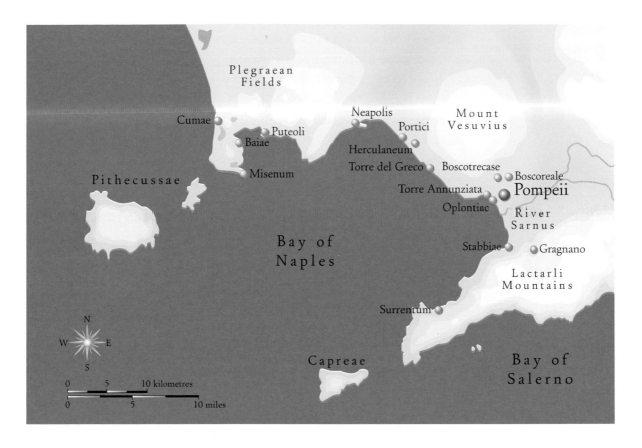

founded by an Italic tribe called the Oscans. At Herculaneum the Oscans established a small fishing village on the high ground between two streams that flowed from the slopes of Mount Vesuvius to the sea, whereas at Pompeii the Oscans built their village on an ancient volcanic lava ridge just behind the later Roman forum in the Regions VII and VIII (see page 88 for an explanation of Giuseppe Fiorelli's plan of Pompeii). The Oscans were probably descended from the prehistoric tribes that hunted and fished in this part of Italy. Their language was used by later peoples and examples appear as graffiti on the walls of Pompeii and Herculaneum.

In the sixth century BC Greek traders were in close contact with both Pompeii and Herculaneum, taking advantage of their strategic position on the important trade route between the Greek settlements of Paestum and Cumae and beyond. Greek culture and commerce gradually assimilated and replaced the original Oscan communities of both towns.

Greek influence can be seen in the very name of the town, Hercula-neum, derived from the Greek god Hercules, the son of Jupiter and

The Bay of Naples in the Roman period. Misenum naval base, and home of the Plinys, had a grandstand view of the horrors that took place at Pompeii and Herculaneum, just across the bay and less than ten kilometres from Vesuvius.

Alcmene. Alcmene was mortal and the goddess Juno, Jupiter's jealous wife, enraged at the birth of Hercules, sent two mythical serpents to kill him as he lay sleeping in his cradle. The infant Hercules woke and strangled both serpents, thus thwarting Juno's plans. Later, Juno schemed for Hercules, now a young man, to undertake a series of life-threatening challenges – the Twelve Labours of Hercules. The first was to kill a lion that was terrorising the people of Nemea and could not be overcome with any conventional weapon. Hercules killed it with his bare hands, then skinned the animal using its own claws. From then on he wore the lion's pelt and is shown thus in many statues. Having completed all twelve labours, Hercules entered the Pantheon of Greek gods as a demi-god. This original Greek myth of Hercules was later adopted by the Romans, who portrayed him as a bearded, middle-aged prizefighter with more than his fair share of human foibles rather than as a fit young man as the Greeks did.

The origin of the name Pompeii is more prosaic and probably derived from the Oscan word '*pompe*', meaning 'five'. This might indicate that five different ethnic groups could be found at Pompeii, or it could have the more mundane meaning of a hand, presumably offered in friendship and trade. It is not known who controlled sixth-century Pompeii; as the Oscan influence decreased, both Greeks and Etruscans came to the area and arte-facts from both cultures have been found. Strabo, the first-century-BC Roman geographer, does not even mention the Greeks in his account of the

According to legend, Hercules, returning from Spain, stepped ashore at the future town of Herculaneum. He made a sacrifice to the gods and the spot came to be named after him.

history of Pompeii before the Romans: 'The Oscans held Herculaneum and the neighbouring Pompeii, in the vicinity of the Sarno River, after them it was held by the Etruscans and the Pelasgians, and later still by the Samnites, who were finally driven out by the Romans.' (Strabo, 5.4.8). The Pelasgians were a local mythical tribe and it may be a name given to all ethnic people in the vicinity. The period of co-existence between the Etruscans and the Greeks came to an end in 474 BC, when the Etruscan navy was destroyed in a decisive battle by a Greek fleet from Syracuse: the Greeks now ruled the Gulf of Naples from the fortified acropolis of Cumae. At Pompeii temples were restored and the town was refortified with a surrounding wall, built of lava

Ancient Doric columns that surround an even older sacred well. The function of the well was to supply sacred water to the nearby temples.

blocks sheathed in rectangular blocks of limestone from the Sarno valley, and square towers and gateways. Pompeii was a maritime outpost, allowing the Greeks to utilise the site's excellent strategic position on a spur overlooking the River Sarno and the landing place by the sea. Here the Greeks built the Temple of Apollo on a mound overlooking the main routes into the city. Another Greek shrine was built on the south-eastern slopes surrounded by a wall of volcanic rock blocks. This shrine, later known as the 'Triangular Forum', was dedicated to Minerva and Hercules, who may have become associated with the foundation of Pompeii as well as of Herculaneum.

Aerial photograph which shows the topography of Pompeii. Instantly recognisable is the large amphitheatre, capable of seating up to 20,000 spectators and situated in a corner of the ancient town.

Pompeii began to expand and building work started in Region VI. The town was laid out according to the principles of the Greek architect Hippodamus of Miletus, with a regular geometric grid and two entrances on the north side. One was the Vesuvius Gate – the road through it skirted Mount Vesuvius and headed inland – whilst the road through the other, the Herculaneum Gate, followed the coast to Naples via Herculaneum. The road from the Vesuvius Gate exited the city on the southern side at the Stabian Gate and continued to Stabiae. Through the other southern gate, the Nuceria Gate, passed the road to Nuceria. This road seems to have been a spur from the main Stabiae road. Later buildings in the eastern quarter of the city have destroyed all traces of the early road to Nuceria. This Greek city layout persisted right through to AD 79, despite the fact that Pompeii was conquered by the Samnites.

THE SAMNITE INVASION

During the 420s BC, the Samnites swept down from the mountains of Abruzzi and Calabria and conquered most of the Greek colonies around the Bay of Naples. The Samnites then settled on the coastal plains where the people became known as the *Campani* and the region's name of Campania still exists today. They re-adopted the use of the Oscan language and enlarged Pompeii, reinforcing the walls with towers. The Samnite Wars against the Romans see-sawed, with first the Romans and then the Samnites being defeated.

The agricultural boundaries to the north of Pompeii, and as far as Boscoreale, seem to have been laid out with a grid-like regularity from this period. Samnite burial grounds dating from the fourth and third centuries BC have been discovered alongside the roads leading out from the Herculaneum and Stabian Gates. Another Samnite relic found was a public banqueting hall, discovered under a house dating from the second century BC in Region VII. The rooms of the banqueting hall contain ledges on which couches for guests could have been placed. Two other examples of banqueting halls are known, at Buccino and Capua, the principal Samnite town in Campania. These banqueting halls were used by guilds or colleges, the backbone of Samnite social organisation and whose Oscan name is *Vereiia*.

The Romans formed an alliance with the Samnites in Campania but continued to fight them in their mountain homelands until they were defeated in 202 BC. The Roman Republic was now able to extend its influence in Campania and around the coast. It founded numerous colonies, which strengthened its control of the area. Maritime trade revolved around the free port of Delos situated on the island of the same name in the middle of the Aegean Sea. Delos was strategically placed for trade with the newly emerging cities of Italy and the rich and exotic cities of Asia Minor. Pompeii, being situated close to the important port of Puteoli, no doubt took advantage of this to send its products and produce on trading voyages to the east, which was an important market for Pompeii. The house furnishings of Pompeii show eastern influence and eastern religions like the cult of Isis were established at Pompeii and elsewhere in Campania. Despite this thriving eastern trade, Pompeii's allegiance to the Roman Republic was never in doubt. The owner of the House of the Faun had a Latin greeting inscribed on its threshold whilst decorating the interior with a scheme which is clearly Egyptian and Greek in taste and style. The most spectacular example of this is the floor mosaic situated in the second tablinum. Based on the now lost painting by Philoxenos of Eretria, it probably shows Alexander the Great bearing down on the Persian ruler Darius during the Battle of Issus.

Throughout this period Pompeii remained a fortified city that respected its treaty with Rome and resisted Pyrrhus, King of Epirus, in *c.* 280 BC and also Hannibal in 216 BC, unlike most of the other Campanian cities.

Found in a house on Via dell' Abbondanza, this wonderful ivory statuette portrays the Indian goddess Lakshmi, who was the goddess of beauty and fertility.

However, in March 90 BC the Samnite towns of Campania rebelled against Rome and so did Pompeii. Sulla led the Roman armies that besieged Pompeii and battered its walls with huge stone balls whose marks remain today.

POMPEII UNDER ROMAN RULE

By the autumn of 89 BC the city had been taken by Sulla's Roman troops and later, in 80 BC Sulla's nephew Publius was tasked with founding a colony at Pompeii – *Colonia Cornelia Veneria Pompeianorum*. The event was commemorated by the construction of the Temple of Venus on the south-eastern spur of the city. The temple, of white marble, overlooked and dominated the road leading into the city from the landing place at the mouth of the River Sarno. Built in the Roman Corinthian style, it heralds a change in building techniques and decoration at Pompeii.

The agricultural land of Pompeii's nobility was given to 2,000 Roman soldiers from Sulla's army. This new Roman colony at Pompeii must have transformed every aspect of society. Certainly houses like the Villa of the Mysteries, the Villa of Cicero and the Villa of Diomedes were rebuilt and decorated with frescoes in what is known as the second style, which dates to the years immediately after 80 BC. The houses that retained decorations in the first style, such as the House of the Faun, may indicate that Samnite ownership continued after the Roman conquest.

Roman Architecture and Culture

Radical changes to the layout of the public buildings in the city reflect the new tastes and requirements of the Romans. The old Triangular Forum became part of the theatre complex. A covered theatre (*odeion*) was built and plays in Latin performed there, whilst the larger open-air theatre still put on plays in Oscan. The establishing of public baths was also high on the agenda. The Forum Baths were built and the Stabian Baths, although dating from the Samnite period, were refurbished. Temples were built: the Temple of Zeus Meilichios dates from this period, and there were additions to the Temple of Apollo, but the grandest scheme was the rebuilding of the Temple of Jupiter. Situated on the northern side of the Forum, the temple was rebuilt to accommodate the cult of the Capitoline triad: Jupiter, Juno and Minerva. The Capitolium was present in all Roman colonies because it was considered to be the transposition of the main state deities, to whom Rome's Capitoline temple was dedicated.

The largest building project at this time was the construction of the amphitheatre, paid for by two of Sulla's commanders, Gaius Quinctius Valgus and Marcus Porcius, during their one-year term as town magistrates. This is the oldest known Roman amphitheatre, dating from 70 BC. It could hold 20,000 spectators, which suggests that not only the people of Pompeii but also those living in the surrounding district could attend the games. In AD 59 the amphitheatre witnessed fighting between spectators from Pompeii and their neighbours from Nuceria, with whom they had

The curved stairway leading to the seats in the odeion theatre. Two kneeling *telamones* support a stone shelf with their elbows whilst the low wall that separates the *ima cavea* from the *media cavea* terminates in two winged griffins.

a score to settle as Nuceria had recently become a Roman colony and had taken over part of Pompeii's territory. Tacitus recorded the unpleasant affair:

> There was a serious fight between the inhabitants of two Roman settlements, Nuceria and Pompeii. It arose out of a trifling incident at a gladiatorial show given by Livineius Regulus. During an exchange of taunts – characteristic of these disorderly country towns – abuse led to stone throwing, and then swords were drawn. The people of Pompeii, where the show was held, came off best. Many wounded and mutilated Nucerians were taken to the capital. Many bereavements, too, were suffered by parents and children. The Emperor instructed the senate to investigate the affair. The senate passed it to the consuls. When they reported back, the senate debarred Pompeii from holding any similar gathering for ten years. Illegal associations in the town were dissolved, and the sponsor of the show and his fellow instigators of the disorder were exiled. (*Annals*, 14.17)

The ban was only revoked following the disastrous earthquake of AD 62.

The forum was restructured from the old market square of the Samnite city. The forum was the political and civil centre of a Roman city; where everything of civic importance took place. At Pompeii the Temples of Apollo and Jupiter were set up on the western and northern sides of the square, the latter being embellished with equestrian statues and triumphal arches to celebrate successive emperors. The eastern side of the forum continued the '*Pax Romana*' theme with temples to Vespasian, the public Lares and the Eumachia, an enigmatic building whose function was no doubt connected with the imperial family. Imperial connections are attested by the statue of Concordia with the face of Livia, wife of Augustus and the mother of Tiberius. There was also epigraphic evidence celebrating Romulus, the mythical founder of Rome, and Aeneas, reputed to have founded the Julian family to which the Emperor Augustus belonged. The Roman forum was extended north as far as the junction between the Road of Fortune and the Road of Mercury, where another triumphal arch, probably dedicated to Caligula, is to be found. Located here was the Temple of Fortuna Augusta, built by Marcus Tullius on his family's land. He belonged to the famous Tullia family and one of his relatives could have been Cicero, who was assassinated, but whose death Octavian, the future Emperor Augustus, did nothing to prevent. The building of the temple so close to the Roman Forum suggests the Tullia family had been reconciled with the Emperor Augustus.

The main square of the city, repaved and rebuilt in white limestone, was closed to traffic and lined with the most important religious, political and commercial buildings. Numerous pedestals have survived around the square, which would have supported statues of Pompeii's leading citizens, whilst the monumental plinths along the south side of the forum in front of the municipal offices displayed statues of the emperor in a *quadriga* (his four-horse chariot) and other members of the imperial family. Midway along the western side there is a raised dais for orators. None of these statues has been found, suggesting they were salvaged by the Romans soon after the eruption of Mount Vesuvius in AD 79 or had been removed earlier.

Water was an essential ingredient of Roman urban life. At Pompeii a new aqueduct was built linking with the earlier one, which carried water from the Sarno River to the Roman imperial fleet port at Misenum. The *castellum,* or water tower, was built near the Vesuvius Gate, the highest part of the city. From here lead pipes ran to 43 public fountains situated at street corners around the city. The thermal baths of Pompeii were rejuvenated by this abundance of water. The oldest of these, the Stabian Baths, had new stucco decorations added. The Forum Baths were redecorated and new baths were built outside the Maritime Gate. Some homeowners took advantage of the new water supply and built suites of private baths, some of which, such as those at the Villa of Julia Felix, were

A detail of the beautiful stucco decoration to be found in the public baths of Pompeii. The walls were decorated with elegant, slender Corinthian columns with highly decorated capitals.

occasionally opened to the public. Other houses utilised the water supply to adorn their gardens with fountains and waterfalls.

THE IMPACT OF THE GREAT EARTHQUAKE

On 5 February AD 62 or AD 63, disaster struck Pompeii and Herculaneum. The Roman philosopher Seneca describes the event:

> Pompeii, the famous city in Campania, has been laid low by an earthquake which also disturbed all the adjacent districts. The city is in a pleasant bay, some distance from the open sea, and bounded by the shores of Surrentum [Sorrento] and Stabiae on one side and of Herculaneum on the other; the shores meet there. In fact it occurred in days of winter, a season which, our ancestors used to claim, was free from such disaster. This earthquake was on the Nones of February, in the consulship of Regulus and Verginius. It caused great destruction in Campania, which had never been safe from this danger but had never been damaged, and time and again had got off with a fright. Also, part of the town of Herculaneum is in ruins, and even the structures which are left are shaky. The colony of Nuceria escaped destruction but still has much to complain about. Naples also lost many private dwellings but no public buildings, and was only mildly grazed by the great disaster, but some villas collapsed, others here and there shook without damage. To these calamities others were added: they say that a flock of hundreds of sheep was killed, statues were cracked, and some people were so shocked that they wandered about as if deprived of their wits. (*Naturales Quaestiones*, VI)

Herculaneum had been almost completely destroyed, Pompeii badly damaged, and the most urgent task was to rebuild the cities. The export of wine, woollen goods and *garum* was increased. Pompeii and Herculaneum were both situated in an agricultural paradise. The fertile slopes of Vesuvius were covered with vines and olive trees and the cultivation of spelt, a variety of durum wheat, was profitable because farmers could obtain at least two harvests a year. Sheep breeding was flourishing and the elite families employed hundreds of craftsmen to turn the raw wool into fine cloth and the Eumachia was probably where it was sold. Another lucrative export was *garum,* an evil-smelling fish sauce. Trade in *garum* was in the hands of prosperous Pompeian families, such as the Umbricii. The quality of the sauce depended on the fish used: tuna, mackerel and moray eel for the more expensive varieties, and anchovies for a coarser type sold in the bars.

Commerce was very important in Pompeii and odes to profit were included in the fabric of some buildings. *Lucrum gaudium,* 'profit is joy', is the motto inscribed around the edge of the impluvium in one house, other entrance halls have mosaic inscriptions announcing – *Salve lucru,* 'welcome to profit'. Statues of Mercury, the god of commerce, abound.

For the leading Pompeian families trade was booming. Pompeii was classified as an emporium, or entrepôt, because it had a port. Wine had been shipped to Gaul and around the Mediterranean from the first century BC. The Pompeiian traders had built a complex network of agents throughout the Roman world and beyond, reaching as far as Egypt, Africa, Asia and even India. The extent of this trade can be gauged from the survival of over 150 writing tablets from the house of the Pompeiian banker Lucius Caecilius Jucundus. The house was damaged in the earthquake of AD 62 but contained financial receipts since AD 52. The wooden tablets had originally been covered with a thin film of wax but the stylus had scored into the wooden base, thus preserving the written accounts. Jucundus acted just like a modern bank, lending money to merchants in return for a fee and no doubt interest on the loan.

Prior to the earthquake of AD 62 the population of Pompeii has been estimated at between 10,000 and 15,000 people. The rich and poor lived in harmony just as the Greeks, Etruscans, Oscans and Latins had done in previous centuries. The city had experienced no interclass strife or racial discrimination. Slave and master co-existed in social harmony. Pompeii seemed untouched by the political power struggles that preceded the reign of Augustus. It was prosperous and gradually the town walls lost their importance and other structures were built over them. Although the earthquake of AD 62 left many of the buildings in ruins, restoration work started almost immediately and much was accomplished, especially in private homes.

The bronze head of the banker Lucius Caecilius Jucundus (or his father) found in his house in Pompeii.

Fourth-style paintings from Pompeii illustrating the various processes employed in fulleries. Above, a worker is carding a tunic whilst a second worker carries a cane cage on which cloth is stretched to be bleached by sulphur steam. Below, workers tread the dirt out of clothes using a mixture of urine, soda and water.

Remains of the Temple of Isis, completely rebuilt following the earthquake of AD 62, and subsequently destroyed by the eruption of AD 79. Its remains created a sensation when discovered in the eighteenth century.

These earthquakes had brought Pompeii and Herculaneum close to total collapse. Some of the leading citizens left for safer areas. Property was sold at very low prices to the brave souls who remained. It was economic to buy a house, demolish it and turn it into gardens. A period of social unrest followed the earthquakes to the extent that the Emperor Vespasian sent one of his magistrates, Suedius Clemens, from Rome to restore order. Those who had taken occupancy of public property were punished and their land confiscated. Pompeii became a huge building site. Many of the larger houses were sub-divided and roughly repaired. Some were converted for commercial or industrial uses, such as the house converted into a fuller's workshop, the Fullonica Stephani. However, the water supply was repaired and reconstruction work started on public buildings such as the Temple of Isis and the Temple of Vespasian. Restored houses were decorated in a new style, the so-called fourth style. The new-found enthusiasm was cut short by the disastrous eruption of Vesuvius on 24 August AD 79.

The town was buried under 6 metres (20 feet) of volcanic debris; it never recovered and became a tomb.

LIFE BEFORE DEATH

Sunrise on 24 August in the year AD 79 was no different from that of any other hot summer's day in Campania. The Bay of Naples was blue and glassy calm. Mount Vesuvius was clothed with the greenery of olive trees and vineyards. The citizens of Pompeii and Herculaneum woke early to make the most of the daylight. The master of the house or his steward would stir the slaves into action, as, whip in hand, he shouted: 'Sweep the pavement! Polish up the pillars! Down with that dusty spider, web and all! One of you clean the flat silver, another the embossed vessels!'

Opposite The *caldarium*, or hot room, at the Forum Baths. Situated in the apse is the *labrum*, a marble fountain providing cool water to refresh the bathers.

Romans were early risers and, even if a person did not get up straight away, he would attend to writing or correspondence. For the Roman male getting up was usually a speedy and simple task and there was very little luxury in the bedchamber. Furniture was kept to a minimum, usually just the couch that gave the bedroom its name, the *cubiculum*, as well as a chest in which to store clothes, a chair for visitors or secretaries to sit on and of course the bed. However sumptuous it looked, the bed was not comfortable. The sprung base was made of rope woven into webbing. On top of this was placed a mattress and a bolster, which served as a pillow. In poorer houses both were stuffed with straw, whilst in the more opulent establishments wool or even swans' down were used. On top of the mattress were two sheets, between which the Roman slept, and a rich counterpane or quilt. Again, the quality and wealth of the house would be reflected in the costly materials used: the most expensive would be multi-coloured silk from the east, threaded or embroidered with gold. Beside the bed would be a mat, and under the bed would be found the chamber pot or urinal vessel.

The Roman male did not undress to go to bed. He removed his cloak or toga, putting it either on the bed or throwing it over the chair, and removed his sandals. He kept the rest of his clothes on. These comprised a loincloth knotted around the waist and a tunic that consisted of two widths of linen or wool sewn together to make a shirt, which was put on over the head and fastened around the waist with a belt. Different social classes had different styles of tunic. The military tunic was somewhat shorter than that of civilians, whilst the woman's tunic was longer than the man's, sometimes reaching almost to the heels. A Roman senator's tunic was edged with purple. Occasionally, if it was cold, two tunics would be worn, one on top of the other, and if, like Augustus, you felt the cold, you could wear up to four tunics. On top of the tunic was worn the toga.

The toga developed from the cloak, and the name derived from the Latin *tegere,* meaning 'to cover'. Woven out of white wool, the toga comprised a semi-circle of cloth with a diameter of 5.5 metres (18.5 feet). About 2 metres (6.5 feet) of the straight edge was placed over the left shoulder, the curved side being outside; the remaining part of the toga was passed round the body, under the right arm, and then thrown over the left shoulder. The part that hung down in front from the left shoulder was then pulled up under the fold across the body. The toga was a worthy cere-

monial garment for the masters of the world, but it required skill to wear it properly. It was heavy, needed frequent washing, and it was expensive. The toga was not a popular garment to wear, especially in provincial cities such as Pompeii and Herculaneum. Emperors were constantly signing decrees enforcing the wearing of the toga for certain occasions: Claudius for tribunals, Domitian for the theatre, and Commodus for the amphitheatre.

At Pompeii, as elsewhere in Campania, a popular form of dress was the *pallium*, a simpler form of Greek garment. In some cases, particularly for those living in the countryside, the only time a Roman citizen wore the toga was on his deathbed, the satirist Juvenal claimed. It was said that Vespasian could put on his toga unaided in less than a minute and be ready for his imperial duties.

Roman men seldom washed in the morning, but attended the baths in the early afternoon after business had finished. Breakfast was a simple affair, occasionally just a glass of water, but more usually fruit, freshly baked bread or honey. After cleaning his teeth the Roman male was ready for his day.

A typical Roman bedroom, or *cubiculum*, with a highly ornate couch for sleeping. There would be no other furniture, the room being highly decorated with wall paintings and floor mosaics.

ROMAN WOMEN AND STYLE

If married, the Roman woman either slept in a room on her own or shared a room with her husband. This seems to have been a matter of choice or social status; the married couple made their choice depending on their inclination and the bedroom space available. Roman aristocrats could organise their sleeping arrangements in such a way that man and wife could sleep apart and be attended by their own slaves. Pliny the Younger woke 'round about the first hour, rarely earlier, rarely later', and found himself 'wonderfully free and abstracted from those outward objects that dissipate attention and left to my own thoughts.' (*Epistles,* 1.IX.36) A Roman wife, like her husband, kept on her undergarments at night: 'Her loin clothe, brassiere, corset, tunic and occasionally to the annoyance of her husband a mantle over all'. Like her husband, she left bathing to the afternoon. She would dress in a long dress called a *stola.* When she went out later she might add a shawl (*palla*), and have a slave in attendance holding a parasol above her head as protection against the sun. She might also avail herself of a fan to keep away the mid-summer flies.

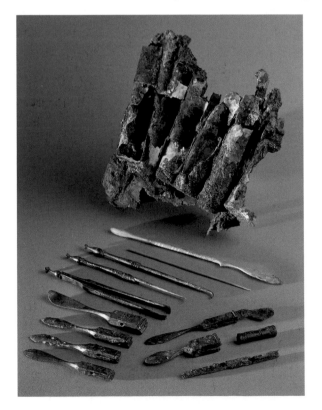

A make-up case from Pompeii, complete with cosmetic instruments and compartments for make-up, powder and creams.

The most important task for the Roman woman was dressing her hair. A special slave called the *ornatrix* was trained in the hairstyle of the day. All over the empire Roman women emulated the coiffures of the Roman imperial family. Even on the very edge of empire, at Vindolanda in northern Britain, the commander's wife wrote in a letter: 'I enclose a coin that shows the latest coiffure of our beloved empress. I have had my hair done like it and pass it on to you'. By AD 79 the simplicity of the republican hairstyle had disappeared to be replaced on occasion by complicated high-piled coiffures. Juvenal writes sarcastically on how extravagant women's hairstyles could be: 'So numerous are the tiers and storeys piled one upon another on her head! In front you would take her for an Andromache; she is not so tall behind; you would not think it was the same person.' (*The Sixteen Satires*, 6.501–4)

Aristocratic Pompeiian women surrounded by a crowd of slaves choosing their clothes and having their hair and make-up attended to.

Once the hair was dressed, the slave then applied her mistress's make-up. This consisted of white chalk powder to the forehead and arms, red ochre to the cheeks, black charcoal rubbed into the eyebrows and eyelids, and a selection of perfumes to complete the 'toilet'. A number of make-up cases have survived from Pompeii and Herculaneum and are on display in the Archaeological Museum in Naples. These little boxes would accompany a Roman woman throughout the day, for making up in the morning and after bathing and finally for removing make-up before retiring at night.

Once made up, the Roman woman would choose her jewellery. Again many examples are on display in Naples. Multiple earrings could be worn, a jewelled collar or necklace, bracelets, and a variety of brooches and finger rings. If she was of high rank, the hem of her *stola* would be embroidered with gold. The *stola* was gathered in at the waist by a belt and a *palla* would be draped over her shoulders – held in place with a *fibula*, a brooch shaped like a safety pin, which was both ornament and fastener.

Women's dress in Pompeii and Herculaneum would be distinguished by the brilliance of the colours. The preferred material was silk, imported annually from India. Romans were obsessed with the east, and with the successful conquests there under Augustus, the Silk Road was now open. Pompeiian merchants used a variety of natural dyes to enhance the original colours of the silk: saffron for yellow, woad for blue, madder for red, oak gallnuts for black, salt of tartar for white. The ladies of Pompeii and Herculaneum would have taken advantage of these multi-coloured robes and shawls and literally shone in the bright Mediterranean sunshine.

MEN AND WOMEN IN SOCIETY

In her Campanian household a Roman woman held the respected position of mistress. Whilst servants and slaves handled most of the chores, they, in turn, were managed by the mistress of the house. The husband's *patria potestas* (paternal authority), or that of his father if still head of the family, gave him life-or-death authority over his children. Unwanted newborn children were at worst thrown on the public rubbish dumps, or at best sold into slavery. The absolute family authority of *patria potestas* was still lawful until AD 317.

Roman women usually married between the ages of 13 and 17. Until the late republic most marriages were of the so-called *manus* type. This entailed the woman leaving the *patria potestas* of her own family and transferring herself and her property to her husband's *patria potestas*. There were serious disadvantages in this system, both to herself and to her family. She would no longer have access to her own wealth, and if she died, her own family would be excluded from any inheritance. The more typical marriage at Pompeii and Herculaneum excluded *manus* and was a marriage by contract before witnesses. This allowed the woman to retain her property and, more importantly, allowed her, by a declaration of will, to divorce her husband. This new type of marriage destroyed the old concept of Roman patriarchal wedlock and marrying a rich woman could lead to problems, as explained by Martial: 'Why don't I want to marry a richer wife, you ask? Well, I don't want to be wife to my wife, but husband. The married woman, my dear

Priscus, must always be subordinate to her man. Else man and wife can never be a match'. (*Epigrams,* VIII. 12)

As well as legal marriage, there also existed in Pompeii and Hercula-neum a form of living together without legal bonds, the *concubinatus*, which gained in popularity from the time of Augustus. Yet Tacitus and other Roman writers still extolled the Roman ideal of womanhood, the chaste and obedient wife and mother who would bring up the children and

One of the most famous and enduring images from Pompeii, the portrait of a young woman called Sappho, deep in thought and writing a letter to a loved one.

be a loyal companion in good times and bad. Tacitus idealised the ancient principles of motherhood:

> Once upon a time every man's son, born of a chaste mother, was reared not by a bought nurse in her den but at his mother's breast and on her lap. And for her the highest merit was to keep house and look after the children. Moreover, they also chose out an older female relative to whose tried and proven character all the children of a single family could be entrusted. In her presence nobody dared to say what it was not nice to say, or do what it was wrong to do. And she governed not only the lessons and tasks but also the recreation and play of the children with a certain sanctity and reverence... But now the newborn baby is handed over to some little Greek nursemaid, with a man slave for assistant, just picked out of the house mob and often the lowest of the low, fit for no serious duties. From that moment the raw and tender minds are soaked in their fables and superstitions. And not a member of the household minds a bit what he or she says or does in front of the infant master. On the contrary the parents themselves, far from imbuing the little ones with habits of honour and modesty, encourage them in skittishness and frivolity, so that they became gradually filled with impudence and contempt for themselves and others. (*Dialogus de Oratoribus*, 28–9)

In Pompeii and Herculaneum, Roman mothers played a small part in bringing up their children. Their education was also delegated to slaves. There was no state schooling, although Pliny the Younger endeavoured to motivate parents to pay the salary of a teacher by contributing a third of the cost himself (*Epistles*, IV. 13).

DAILY LIFE AND POLITICS

Everyday life outside the cities of Pompeii and Herculaneum can be gauged by extracts from Pliny the Younger's letters:

> You ask how I divide up my day on my country estate in summer. I wake up when I like, mostly at six, often earlier, seldom later... About ten or eleven – I don't keep a strict timetable – I go out to the flower garden or

Toilet and writing utensils were both delicate and prolific. Every Roman woman had a set of each to be able to prepare for the day and to write to her friends.

the covered walk to think... Then I go for a drive. After that I read a Greek or Latin speech, aloud and with emphasis, not so much to exercise my voice as to improve my digestion. Once more I take the air, the oiling, gymnastics, bath. At table when I'm alone with my wife or with a few friends, I have a book read to me. After the meal there's a comedy played or a lyrist performs. Finally I walk in the open air with my people, some of whom are educated. In such a manner, with all kinds of conversations, we pass the evening, and even the longest day draws quickly to a close. (*Epistles,* IX. 36)

24 August, the ninth day before those Kalends of September, was a busy day for both Pompeii and Herculaneum. Augustus had died some 60 years earlier and had been deified. The month August was named for him and for some days there could have been public celebrations. The day before had also been special. It was the feast day in honour of Vulcan, the god of fire and metalworking. Volcanoes, it was believed, were where Vulcan kept his forge. The excitement and activity of the Vulcan celebrations had started early; booths lined the entrance roads to Pompeii and Herculaneum. Townspeople were already enjoying the spectacles of jugglers, fortune-tellers, street musicians and acrobats. In Herculaneum players were rehearsing and in the sports arenas of both towns, athletic events were just starting.

In the grand houses of Pompeii and Herculaneum, the *patronus* would open his office to receive the first of his clients. Patronage was how business worked. Men with ambition would be obliged to seek a patron who could further their career or enhance their social standing. A regular courtesy call to your patron was essential, for the *patronus* was honour-bound to welcome his client to his house, to give advice and make small gifts. There was a strict code of etiquette on such occasions. In Rome it was imperative to wear a toga, although in provincial cities such as Pompeii and Herculaneum this rule would have been relaxed. Clients had to wait their turn and access to the patron was not based on order of arrival but on their social status. When entrance was finally granted it was essential to show due respect and correctly address your patron. Requests could then be made, business introductions facilitated and advice given. The homage offered had strings: loyalty on both sides was the cornerstone of the arrangement. Neither party could appear in court against each other and support for each other in public life was paramount.

During working hours the courts of justice would be in session, town councils would be meeting and priestly colleges preparing for the day's activities. It was essential to be involved in these activities, to be informed, to look after the interests of your own friends and clients to gain the respect of your peers and neighbours.

The basilica at Pompeii was one of the most important public buildings in the city. It was where the administration of justice was conducted by the court, presided over by the *duoviri*. The political and administrative institutions were the *ordo decurionum*, the magistrates of the city and the *populus*. The supreme power lay with the two *duoviri* aided by two further magistrates, the *aediles*. The senior magistrates, the *duoviri,* presided over town council meetings, made legal pronouncements, managed the finances of the city and above all administered justice in the courts held in the basilica. Their colleagues, the *aediles*, were usually younger men given their first opportunity in public life. Hoping to make a good impression, they would zealously administer the water supply, the markets and the police force, and see to the general needs of the city. All four magistrates were elected annually in July and election fever would start early. Fortunately, election notices and slogans have survived in some abundance on the walls of Pompeii. It was not considered good form for the candidate to promote himself; this was left to his clients and patrons. One of the attributes

Part of the frieze in the House of Julia Felix. It shows the porticoes of the Forum embellished with garlands and framing equestrian statues on plinths. A crowd of onlookers are enjoying the amenities of the Forum.

promoted was the aptitude and good moral character of the candidate. So it is understandable that one of Pompeii's leading citizens, C. Julius Polybius, was outraged that Cuculla and Zmyrina, two local prostitutes, had shown their support by painting an election poster on the wall of his street. He demanded that the inscription be erased.

Once the magistrates had finished their year in office they became life members of the council of the decurions (*ordo decurionum*). The council

The frontage of shops along the Via dell' Abbondanza provided space for electoral advertising by either the owners or their customers.

usually comprised the aristocratic elite and numbered about 100 members. The quinquennial *duumviri*, elected every five years, but serving for four, had the right to investigate the financial status and moral aptitude of the members of the council. If these were found wanting, the *duumviri* could recommend dismissal. The *populus* was the citizens who had the right to vote, and this included all adult male citizens, but excluded women, slaves, gladiators and Jews. They elected the magistrates every March ready for them to take office on the following 1 July. Cicero remarked it was more difficult to get into the Pompeii city council than the Senate of Rome itself and Petronius, in his story about Trimalchio at nearby Puteoli, says: 'No one, says this man, gives a damn about the way we're hit by the grain situation. To hell with the *aediles*! They're in with the bakers – you be nice to me and I'll be nice to you. So the little man suffers... This place is going down like a calf's tail!' (*Petronius*, 44)

Almost 3,000 election notices have survived on the walls of Pompeii, and more than half of them are for the election in the last year of the town's existence. All of the trades and industries of Pompeii are represented. These include the guilds of porters, bath-stokers, muleteers, even school children are represented ('Teacher Sema with his boys recommends Julius Simplex for the Job'). The vibrancy and number of election notices show a town alive and well, coping with the earthquake disaster of AD 62 and rebuilding for the future. The candidates themselves had the opportunity to expound their political programme whilst standing on the *suggestum*, the orator's platform situated in the forum.

The winners of the elections had to sponsor public building works and gladiatorial games. Although gladiator helmets have been found at Herculaneum, the amphitheatre has not yet been found. At Pompeii the amphitheatre dates from the early years of the colony, the first half of the first century BC. An inscription found *in situ* records: 'Paid for by the two quinquennial *duumviri*, Caius Quinctius Valgus and M. Porcius', whose inscription found at the amphitheatre reads: 'Caius Quinctius Valgus, son of Caius, and Marcus Porcius, son of Marcus, in their capacity as quinquennial *duumviri*, to demonstrate the honour of the colony, erected this sports complex at their own expense and donated it to the colonists for their perpetual use.' Built in the shape of an ellipse, it backed on to a stretch of the city wall and thirty-five rows of seats accommodated a capacity of 20,000 spectators, segregated according to social status. There are more known amphitheatres in Campania than in any other comparable district in the Roman Empire. The structure at Pompeii, being one of the earliest amphitheatres built, has no underground passages or cells for gladiators. The outer wall contains six large exterior staircases, which gave access to the internal walkway and seating.

There is a doorway at each end of the long axis of the arena. The *Porta Triumphalis* was for the opening ceremony; the other, called the *Porta Libitinensis*, was used to remove dead gladiators and animals.

Over 3,000 election notices have survived from the walls of Pompeii, with more than half for the last election to be held. Other notices announce gladiatorial shows or are just plain graffiti.

GLADIATORS AND ENTERTAINMENT

The gladiators trained and lived in the theatre *quadriporticus,* where wonderful gladiatorial parade armour has been found. Games were organised by Pompeiians such as Cn. Alleius Nigidius Maius, who was proclaimed on posters as 'prince of the impresarios'. Games at Pompeii in AD 79 were held on 4, 8, 9, 10, 11, 12 and 20 April, and on 2, 12, 13, 14, 16 and 31 May. The

This famous wall painting from Pompeii depicts the riot between the citizens of Pompeii and Nuceria in AD 59, as recounted by the Roman historian Tacitus.

walls of the amphitheatre are adorned with painted posters extolling the virtues of the gladiators, similar to the way in which modern pop stars are described. The Thracian Celadus is called the 'hero' and 'heart throb of the girls'. Another poster suggests: 'The net-fighter Crescens is the boss who gives the girls the medicine they need at night.' Others record the outcome of contests: 'Three killed, six spared, nine victorious.' Some say: 'There will be awnings,' referring to the linen shades on wooden poles and controlled by guy ropes to shield the spectators from the fierce rays of the sun.

One of the duties of the two *aediles* was to rent the concessions in the square around the amphitheatre to vendors selling souvenirs, food and drink. Painted signs mark the rented areas: 'Cnaeus Aninius Fortunatus occupies this position with permission of the *aediles*.' Other epigraphic evidence of daily life at the amphitheatre is carved on the parapet opposite the wedges of stone seats. Magistrates, who had donated the seats to the people of Pompeii, had their names carved for posterity on the parapet of the arena facing the seats they had paid for. In the lower terrace, where the town aristocrats sat, the seats were numbered and separated by a red line from those of other social classes. The games could also be watched from the porticoes in the attic storey, where there was standing room only. Normally this area would be reserved exclusively for women and slaves.

Support for the gladiators verged on fanatical. The fracas in AD 59 recounted by Tacitus (see page 16) left some Nucerians killed and badly injured during the games organised by Livineius Regulus, who had already been expelled by the senate in Rome for similar misdemeanours. The senate resolved to close the amphitheatre for ten years and exile Livineius and his fellow instigators. The ten-year ban was later lifted, either because of the earthquake in AD 62 or possibly the intercession of Nero's wife Poppaea, whose family were important citizens of Pompeii, owning the Houses of the Golden Cupid and Menander. Enthusiasm for gladiatorial combat increased, and at Pompeii in AD 62 the *quadriporticus* of the theatre was rebuilt as barracks for the gladiators. Individual cells were built over two floors, while the courtyard was used for daily training. Thousands enjoyed the horrible spectacle of gladiatorial combat. There were few objectors.

The historian Nicolaus of Damascus believed that Rome inherited gladiatorial contests from the Etruscans as part of their funerary rites. Certainly in Rome, prior to the building of the Colosseum by Vespasian, gladiators would fight to the death in the forum as part of the funerary rites of major public figures. In Campania the spectacle was established very early on and could be one of the legacies of the Samnites. Indeed, down to the first century BC the terms 'gladiator' and 'Samnite' were synonymous, and 'Samnite' later became the name of a particular type of gladiator.

Gladiators, named after the sword, the *gladius*, that they carried, were a mixture of condemned criminals and prisoners-of-war. There were also career professionals, slaves, freedmen or volunteers. Mostly men, but occasionally women, they were trained in professional schools. The most famous school

Found in the gladiators' barracks were two wooden boxes full of gladiatorial weapons wrapped in cloth. The bronze helmet is decorated with a palm tree – alluding to victory.

A concert party, as portrayed in a mosaic by Dioscurides of Samos. Two musicians dance to the sound of the tambourine and cymbals whilst a double flute player looks on.

ROMAN BATHS

After the morning's activities it was possible to relax at the four public baths known at Pompeii and the two at Herculaneum. The public baths at Pompeii are the Stabian, Forum, Central and Amphitheatre Baths. At Herculaneum they are the Forum and Suburban Baths. Few houses needed private baths; one unexcavated example at Pompeii, the bathing establishment of M. Crassus Frugi, offered salt-water baths and was also open to the public. Many of the baths were owned and run by the community, others were built and paid for by the emperor. Public baths were noisy and overcrowded, but cheap. The entrance fee was usually about half an *as*, the same price as a glass of wine, although in some years potential magistrates as an inducement to voters would offer free entry, covering the running costs of the baths themselves. Most baths opened at midday with slaves ringing bells in the adjoining streets to drum up trade. By AD 79 it was forbidden for men and women to bathe together, so there must have been either separate sections for men and women or different opening times. Rich and poor jostled for space, and the rich brought their slaves to help with the facilities.

All Roman baths were designed to the same pattern. They comprised a dressing (or undressing) room, and then a series of chambers which would get progressively hotter. Most baths were also equipped with a gymnasium with ball courts and a swimming pool. Before bathing, the citizens would undress in the changing room (*apodyterium*). The changing room at the Stabian Baths had a marble bench running around the walls, and clothes could be left in a series of alcoves around the room. The room was often decorated with wonderful stucco reliefs of cupids, nymphs and floral patterns. Once undressed, the bathers could either partake of the gymnasium or move through to the warm room (*tepidarium*). The floor, supported on pillars, had hollow spaces beneath it to allow the passage of hot air to heat the rooms. Once they had become accustomed to the temperature they could take a lukewarm bath. Next, they went into the hot room (*caldarium*), which was filled with hot steam. The floor, for instance decorated with white mosaic tiles framed by a black strip, would be so hot from the underfloor heating that it was essential to wear wooden sandals. The central heating used in the baths of Pompeii and Hercula-neum is said to have been invented early in the first century BC by Gaius Sergius Orata, although there are earlier examples of central heating to be found in Greece. The hot air from furnaces, fuelled by wood or charcoal, was channelled by underfloor passages to the cavities under the floors of the *caldaria* and *tepidaria*. The air temperature would be about 30°C (86°F), but this could be doubled to about 60°C (140°F) in the sweating room (*laconicum*) by drawing the hot air upwards into similar cavities in the walls. In the hot room at the Stabian Baths there was a rectangular marble pool for hot baths. To increase sweating, which was the intention, cool water could be drunk from a marble basin (*labrum*) situated in the apse.

The room was lit by a swivelling bronze skylight that also acted as a hot-air valve. If the temperature was too hot, the window could be opened. After the hot room, bathers returned to the warm room to be dried, covered in oil, massaged and finally scraped with a strigil by slaves. The last room that the bathers entered was the cold room (*frigidarium*), where they took a cold plunge in the bath (*balneum*).

Soap was not available in the baths since it was not in common use, being used to more often to treat sores and as a hair-dye. Pliny the Elder describes it as 'an invention of the Gauls for giving a reddish tint to the hair' (*Natural History*, XXVIII.191). Bathers were expected to bring or purchase their own oil and soda, scrapers (*strigiles*) and towels. After bathing, the visitors could take a walk under the porticoes and purchase hot drinks to replenish some of their lost fluids. Whilst relaxing they could enjoy watching other clients playing games in the ball courts. One popular game was called *trigon*; this was a ball game for three people in which the players, each posted at the corner of a triangle, threw balls at each other without warning – catching with one hand and throwing with the other. A kind of volleyball was also played with two or four players by knocking a ball over a net with the palm of their hand. Other ball games played include 'hop-ball' and 'ball against the wall'. All these games were a prelude to the bath, as a warm up for the clients. Martial alludes to these pre-bathing games in an epigram that he sent to a philosopher friend who appears to have disdained them: 'No hand-ball, no bladder ball, no feather-stuffed ball makes you ready for the warm bath; nor do you stretch forth squared arms besmeared with sticky ointment, darting to and fro, to snatch the dusty scrimmage-ball.' (*Epigrams*, VII.32)

This magnificent marble statue of Venus, goddess of love, mistress of nature, mother of the universe and patroness of Pompeii is in the Farnese Collection at the Archaeological Museum in Naples.

RELIGION AND WORSHIP

At home or in the street, in private or in public, the lives of the Pompeiians and Herculaneans were inextricably bound up with various religions. Although no temples have yet been uncovered at Herculaneum, at least ten are known at Pompeii. One of the most spectacular is the *Capitolium*, which dominated the north end of the forum. This temple was dedicated to the sacred triad of Jupiter, Juno and Minerva. At the other end of the spectrum are the small shrines found in every household dedicated to a variety of gods. At Herculaneum they tend to feature paintings of Hercules, their legendary founder and the only man (apart from the emperors) who was deified.

At Pompeii the choice of gods in the *lararium*, the household shrine, tends to be more prosaic: Bacchus, the god of wine and good living, *Venus Pompeiana*, the city's official goddess to bring good luck and prosperity, and Fortuna, mistress of the world holding the *cornucopia*, the horn of plenty. Romans believed that all important events in life were divinely activated and that different gods were in charge of particular functions and activities. The worship of particular gods for particular purposes was so obscure that by the time of Augustus some of the meanings were no longer remembered. One of the most venerated goddesses was Vesta, keeper of the eternal fire. Other early gods are Ceres, to be appealed to for growth, Mercury for the success of business transactions and Apollo for the power of healing. The most important god to the Romans was Jupiter Best and Greatest (*Optimus Maximus*).

Roman religion was concerned with success, not with sin. 'Jupiter is called Best and Greatest,' Cicero comments, 'because he does not make us just or sober or wise but healthy and rich and prosperous' (*On the Nature of the Gods*, III.87). Pompeii's two patron divinities, Apollo and Venus, both have splendid temples. The Temple of Apollo stands within its own precinct adjacent to the forum. It can be traced back to the sixth century BC, although the present building was constructed during the reorganisation of the area in the second century BC. The cult of Apollo was the most important in Pompeii, and only relegated when the Roman colonists of Sulla imposed the cult of the Capitoline triad – Jupiter, Juno and Minerva – in 80 BC. The temple was seriously damaged in the earthquake of AD 62, but rebuilding had started before the final volcanic eruption of

AD 79. By then, however, Pompeii had passed into the patronage of Venus. Her temple must have been one of the loveliest in Pompeii. Situated on a terrace overlooking the Marine Gate, the temple could be seen by anybody approaching the city from the south-west; in particular, traders and sailors in the port or on the River Sarno below.

The cult of Venus had ancient and obscure origins in Pompeii. It was originally related to Venus Physica, the goddess of health and sickness, of life and death. Sulla introduced the cult of Venus as the goddess of love and beauty. The name of the colony founded for his Roman army veterans incorporated the goddess's name, *Colonia Cornelia Veneria Pompeianorum*, but she was always more to the Pompeiians than the goddess of love. She can be found everywhere in the town, occasionally described on inscriptions as *Venus fisica*, possibly referring to the Greek word for nature, *physis*. Venus was the good luck charm of the Pompeiians. She can be found on election posters: 'Vote for me, and the Venus of Pompeii will bring success to everything you undertake.' A poster in a shop selling wool shows her on a pillar, untouchable by all, a feeling noted in graffiti scrawled on a wall: 'What is the use of having a Venus if she's made of marble?' She can be found adorning a wall in the House of Venus in the Sea Shell (11.3.3) where she floats in a scallop shell escorted, as always, by her two cupids, a scenario painted with dazzling effect by later Renaissance artists.

Another female deity to be found in Pompeii is the Egyptian goddess Isis. The cult probably appeared around 100 BC and the nearest temple outside Pompeii was at Puteoli. It offered life after death to its converts and, although the temple was situated in an out-of-the-way area close to the theatre district, it gained many converts from the slaves and families of freedmen and eventually took hold in the aristocratic classes of Pompeii. Very little remains of the original temple, which was destroyed by the earthquake of AD 62. It was rebuilt by Numerius Popidius Celsinus, a member of a leading Pompeiian family, who was only a child at the time. The inscription over the door reads: 'Numerius Popidius Celsinus, son of Numerius, paid for the Temple of Isis to be rebuilt from its foundations, which had collapsed as a result of the earthquakes. To repay his generosity, the decurions accepted him into their order free of charge, although he was only six years old.' The inscription informs us that the father of the child, a freedman, unable to hold the highest office in Pompeii, was willing to fund

his son to become what he could never be. It also confirms that the building was so badly damaged that it had to be completely rebuilt and that the focus of religious life was now on the 'fringe' religions rather than the traditional deities. It is also interesting that the decurions were willing to allow a minor to join the *curia*, or ruling body, to enable the temple to be rebuilt.

The worship of Isis was treated with suspicion in official circles because of its associations with Ptolemaic Egypt. After the annexation of Egypt by Augustus in 30 BC, however, attitudes relaxed and by AD 38 Rome itself had a Temple of Isis. The cult of Isis had its own full-time priests, whereas the more official Roman religions did not. The priests held daily ceremonies. Before sunrise the statue of Isis was presented to her seated followers who had gathered outside, shaking the rattle (*sistrum*) in her honour. They remained deep in prayer and contemplation until the sun had risen to be blessed by the gathered worshippers, who also celebrated the resurrection of Osiris, god of the underworld, at the daily rebirth of the sun. At 2 pm a second ceremony was held for the adoration

The wonderful painting of Venus lying in a sea shell, with her cloak acting as a sail or sunshade, named the house in which it is found – the House of Venus in the Sea Shell (11.3.3).

of sacred water from the Nile. Both ceremonies were dazzling, elaborate rituals accompanied by music, chanting and the burning of incense. Unfortunately, on Pompeii's final day the priests' lunch hour was disturbed by the eruption of Vesuvius. They fled, leaving their lunch behind, but taking the temple treasure with them. One of the priests, carrying a bag full of gold coins, died at the corner of the Via dell'Abbondanza. The survivors fled to the Triangular Forum, where two were killed by falling masonry and their sacred emblems and regalia scattered. Those who were left took shelter in a house where one by one they died. The last priest died, axe in hand, as he was attempting to cut through the wall of the house, no doubt after the doors were blocked with falling debris.

One of the cults to be found at Pompeii was to the emperor himself. The imperial cult was the most important cult to Romans as it proclaimed that the Julian emperors were descended from Venus, the lover of Mars and the mother of Romulus. The Augustan peace was the sign of a new age, religion was revived, temples newly built and the concept of the emperor as a god on earth first mooted. Augustus did not go as far as his predecessor, Julius Caesar, who was determined to claim divine status for himself, only to be thwarted by his assassination. Augustus reasserted the divinity of Julius Caesar and reaffirmed that he was Caesar's legitimate successor and heir; he styled himself as *divi filius*, the son of a god, and as Augustus (the reverend). He left the possibility that he was indeed divine to posterity, to be

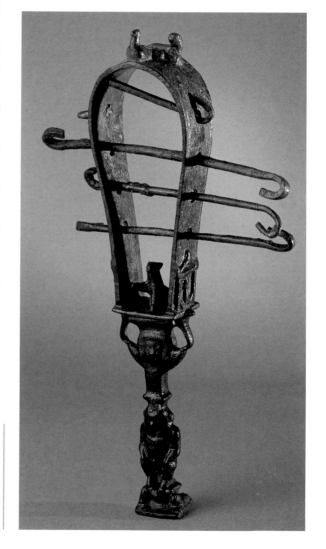

Opposite The Egyptian goddess Isis receiving adoration from her followers. A priest descends the temple steps holding a container of the sacred Nile water.

Right A metal rattle, or *sistrum*, was used by the priests of Isis to drown out any extraneous sounds intruding into the elaborate rituals of the cult.

decided after his death in the light of his earthly achievements. In Rome, Augustus ensured that, rather than direct worship to himself, indirect worship could be promoted if his title 'Augustus' was added to those of divinities who had virtues that he wished to be associated with. The concept was copied throughout the towns, small and large, of the empire.

At Pompeii the first temple built in this manner was the Temple of Fortuna Augusta. The following inscription can be found on the architrave: 'Marcus Tullius, son of Marcus, *duumvir*, with judicial power three times, quinquennalis, *augur* and military tribune elected by the people, erected the Temple of Fortuna Augusta on his land at his own expense.' The Tullia family followed Sulla to Pompeii and frequently held high office in the town. Marcus Tullius was *duumvir* three times and quinquennalis once. The office of military tribune of the people could be awarded only by the emperor, enabling the recipient to attain the rank of knight. After the temple was built, Marcus Tullius would have formed the College of Priests (*Ministri Fortunae Augustae*) for the cult, who, with proper authorisation would donate a statue of Fortune and a statue to every new emperor. Inscriptions in the temple refer to Augustus, Tiberius, Caligula, Claudius and Nero. No inscriptions to new emperors postdate the earthquake of AD 62 when the temple was badly damaged. The temple was built in the last years of the first century BC at the busy crossroads between the Via del Foro and Via di Nola. Anybody arriving from Naples or Herculaneum along the main streets would suddenly have been confronted by the sight of the magnificent white-marble-faced temple decorated with Corinthian columns and capitals. The earthquake destroyed most of the building and very little repair work was carried out. It is believed that architectural material from the temple might have been used for repairs elsewhere; in particular, decorative marble slabs found their way to the Temple of Vespasian.

Construction of new temples for the imperial cult brought advancement opportunities to the local officials – by associating themselves with the imperial cult some of that glory would reflect on them. Other buildings facing the forum square also had links with the cult of the emperor. A statue of the seated emperor modelled as Jupiter was located on a plinth in the centre of the exedra in the covered market. To the south of the market, old shops were demolished to enable two new buildings to be constructed. Both were associated with the imperial cult, as too was the sanctuary of the Lares (*Lares Publici*) which housed the protectors of the town, who have been identified with the deified spirits of dead ancestors. It was thought that the sanctuary was badly damaged by the earthquake in AD 62, and its marble stripped for decoration elsewhere, but recent work by archaeologist John Dobbins suggests the sanctuary was not designed and built until after the earthquake.

To the right of the sanctuary of the Lares is the so-called Temple of Vespasian, who died only one month before the final eruption of Vesuvius. The magnificent altar in the centre of the unroofed area of the temple is carved on all four sides with relief decoration. The face one sees on entering represents an imperial sacrifice, and shows a veiled priest and his assistant, an attendant, flute player and other spectators. Oak wreaths and laurel branches bestowed by the Roman senate on Augustus are also portrayed on the altar.

On that final day in August AD 79 both Pompeii and Herculaneum were busy, functioning towns. The baths were packed, the snack bars open, and athletic events were taking place. Players were rehearsing in the theatres, town council business was being attended to, religious ceremonies happening, bars, brothels and bakers' shops all busy with customers. In the grand houses lunch was being prepared. Tables were set in shaded courtyards or gardens with fountains splashing. In one house overlooking the harbour slaves were about to serve hard-boiled eggs, bread, salad, small cakes and fruit.

Suddenly their world was transformed. The earth shook; the daylight disappeared to be replaced by a night blacker and thicker than any ordinary night. It was the end of their world.

ACTS OF THE GODS

Mount Vesuvius is part of a great chain of volcanoes stretching along Italy from Tuscany down to Sicily and the nearby Lipari Islands (known in the Roman period as the Aeolian or Vulcanion Islands). Vesuvius, Epomeo, Stromboli, Vulcano and Etna are all active volcanoes. The peak of Vesuvius is about 10 kilometres (6 miles) from Pompeii and 7 kilometres (4 miles) from Herculaneum. In 1883 Mount Epomeo, on the island of Ischia in the Bay of Naples, erupted and destroyed the neighbouring towns and villages. Nearby, on the mainland, are the Phlegrean Fields, an area of volcanic activity with bubbling springs and the occasional blast of steam.

Opposite An eighteenth-century artist's impression of Vesuvius erupting. The volcano is part of the great chain of active volcanoes stretching down the length of Italy from Tuscany to Sicily.

Vesuvius, the only active volcano on mainland Europe, is east of Pozzuoli (Puteoli). The whole area around Pozzuoli today is on the move through a process of bradyseism, where volcanic activity is lifting or sinking the ground. Its effects can be seen just off the coast where extensive remains of Roman buildings that once stood on dry land are now underwater.

Vesuvius's is about 1,200 metres (3,937 feet) high and is divided into two peaks, Monte Vesuvio and Monte Somma. However, in the Roman period it was believed that the volcano was extinct. Strabo, the geographer, writing early in the first century AD is the first surviving source to reveal an awareness that Vesuvius had once been active, and noted how fertile the area was:

The great destruction caused by Vesuvius is apparent in the town of Pompeii where temples, basilicas and public baths were utterly destroyed by the eruption in AD 79.

Above these places towers Mount Vesuvius, wholly occupied by beautiful fields all around, except on the summit, the summit itself is mainly flat but wholly sterile, with an ashy appearance; it has cavities with cracks opening in the rocks, which are sooty on the surface as it was devoured by flames. Thus some may suppose that this place once burned and had craters of fire that later died out when the combustible material was used up. This may be the reason for the fertility of the surrounding land as in the case of Catania, where it is said that the soil covered with ash thrown out by the fire of Etna is particularly suitable for vine growing. (*Geographica*, V.48)

Virgil too mentions the excellent wine produced by the vines on the slopes of Mount Vesuvius, as well as olive trees, good plough land and grazing for sheep (*Georgics*, 11.224). A painting that may portray Vesuvius was found in the shrine (*lararium*) of the House of the Centenary (IX.8.5). It portrays the god Bacchus, amongst a luxuriant cluster of grapes with his *thyrsus* (banner) and panther next to a mountain covered in trellised vine-yards. Further up the slope is land for grazing and woodland, and a large serpent painted in front of the mountain represents the fertility of the soil.

ACTS OF THE GODS – THE EARTHQUAKES AND ERUPTION

On 5 February AD 62 a serious earthquake occurred, affecting the entire region. Pompeii and Herculaneum were both severely damaged, the moment of destruction being shown dramatically on two stone reliefs that Lucius Caecilius Jucundus put up on his house shrine at Pompeii (V.I.26). The reliefs portray the public buildings on the north side of the forum at Pompeii during the earthquake. The Temple of Jupiter is shown collapsing in the middle of the relief, while a sacrifice is being offered on the right, no doubt to avert further tremors. Repair work started almost immediately in both cities, but the following years may have seen further tremors. Seventeen years later, on 24 August AD 79, the mountain erupted into life.

Pliny the Younger had recorded that there had been several small earthquakes in the days before, but the eruption on 24 August appears to have been heralded by a single small blast in the early hours of the morning. It is likely that people would have heard it and wondered what it was, especially if, as is likely, it was accompanied by a small earthquake that rattled windows and doors. The explosion deep inside Vesuvius would have disgorged a dark column of ash, which would have climbed upwards above the crater to a height of almost 2 kilometres (1^1/$_2$ miles). It created a billowing cloud that began to fall as fine ash on the east side of Vesuvius. The ash did not come from fresh hot magma rock, but was the remains of the old magma blocking the vent. The explosion was caused by the hot magma rising deep inside the volcano and turning the water-filled rock inside the volcano to super-heated steam. The effect, not unlike a cork escaping from a champagne bottle, created a cloud of condensed steam mixed with ash, which lingered until the main eruption some hours later.

At 1 pm the main eruption started. It has been described in some detail by Pliny the Younger, a friend of the Emperor Trajan and the nephew of Pliny the Elder who was admiral of the Roman fleet at the port of Misenum. In AD 104 the younger Pliny wrote two letters to the historian Tacitus describing what he had seen all those years previously:

My uncle was stationed at Misenum in active command of the fleet.
The ninth day before the Calends of September [24 August], in the early afternoon, my mother drew to his attention a cloud of unusual size and appearance. He had been out in the sun, had taken a cold bath, eaten a light lunch while lying down, and was then working at his books. He called for his shoes and climbed up to a place that would give him the best view of the phenomenon. It was not clear at that distance from which mountain the cloud was rising (it was afterwards known to be Vesuvius). Its general appearance can best be expressed as being like an umbrella pine, for it rose to a great height on a sort of trunk and then split off into branches. I imagine because it was thrust upwards by the first blast and then left unsupported as the pressure subsided, or else it was borne down by its own weight so that it spread out and gradually dispersed. In places it looked white, elsewhere blotched and dirty, according to the amount of soil and ashes it carried with it. My uncle's scholarly acumen saw at once that it was important enough for a closer inspection, and he ordered a boat to be made ready, telling me I could come with him if I wished. I replied that I preferred to go on with my studies and as it happened he had himself given me some writing to do.
As he was leaving the house he was handed a message from Rectina, wife of Tascius, whose house was at the foot of the mountain so that

escape was impossible except by boat. She was
terrified by the danger threatening her and
implored him to rescue her from her fate. He
changed his plans, and what he had begun in a
spirit of enquiry he completed as a hero. He
gave orders for the warships to be launched and
went on board himself with the intention of
bringing help to many more people beside
Rectina, for this lovely stretch of coast was
thickly populated.

He hurried to the place where everyone else
was hastily leaving, steering his course straight
for the danger zone. He was entirely fearless,
describing each new movement and phase of the
portent to be noted down exactly as he observed
them. Ashes were already falling, hotter and
thicker as the ships drew near, followed by bits
of pumice and blackened stones, charred and
cracked by the flames: then suddenly they were

Pliny the Elder
(Plinius Secundus,
AD 23–79), famous for
his encyclopedia and his
death (above) at Stabiae
during the eruption of
Vesuvius in AD 79.

in shallow water, and the shore was blocked by the debris from the
mountain. For a moment my uncle wondered whether to turn back, but
when the helmsman advised this he refused, telling him that Fortune
stood by the courageous and they must make for the home of
Pomponianus at Stabiae. He was cut off there by the breadth of the bay
(for the shore gradually curves round a basin filled by the sea) so that he
was not as yet in danger, though it was clear that this would come nearer
as it spread. Pomponianus had therefore already put his belongings on
board ship, intending to escape if the contrary wind fell. The wind was of
course full in my uncle's favour, and he was able to bring his ship in. He
embraced his terrified friend, cheered and encouraged him, and thinking
he could calm his fears by showing his own composure, gave order that
he was to be carried to the bathroom.

After his bath he lay down and dined; he was quite cheerful, or at any
rate he pretended he was, which was no less courageous.

Meanwhile on Mount Vesuvius broad sheets of fire and leaping flames
blazed at several points, their bright glare emphasised by the darkness of
night. My uncle tried to allay the fears of his companions by repeatedly

declaring that these were nothing but bonfires left by the peasants in their terror, or else empty houses on fire in the districts they had abandoned.

Then he went to rest and certainly slept, for as he was a stout man his breathing was rather loud and heavy and could be heard by people coming and going outside his door. By this time the courtyard giving access to his room was full of ashes mixed with pumice-stones, so that its level had risen, and if he had stayed in the room any longer he would never have got out. He was wakened, came out and joined Pomponianus and the rest of the household, who had stayed up all night. They debated whether to stay indoors or take their chance in the open, for the buildings were now shaking with violent shocks, and seemed to be swaying to and fro as if they were torn from their foundations. Outside, on the other hand, there was the danger of falling pumice-stones, even though these were light and porous; however after comparing the risks they chose the latter. In my uncle's case one reason outweighed the other, but for the rest it was a choice of fears. As a protection against falling objects they put pillows on their heads tied down with cloths.

Elsewhere there was daylight by this time, but they were still in darkness, blacker and denser than any ordinary night, which they relieved by lighting torches and various kinds of lamps. My uncle decided to go down to the shore to see at first hand whether it was possible to escape by sea; but they found the waves still wild and dangerous. There a sheet was spread on the ground for my uncle to lie down, and he called repeatedly for cold water, which he drank. Then the

One of the more famous kinds of lamp found by excavators in the Temple of Venus at Pompeii, it was probably donated by Nero and his wife Poppaea. Solid gold, it has a reservoir of olive oil and two wicks.

flames and smell of sulphur that heralded the approaching fire drove the others to take flight. Roused, my uncle struggled to his feet, leaning on two slaves, but immediately collapsed. I assume that his breathing was impeded by the dense fumes, which blocked his windpipe – for it was constitutionally weak and narrow, and often inflamed. When daylight returned – two days after the last time he had seen it – his body was found intact and uninjured, still fully clothed as in life. He looked more like a sleeper than a dead man. (*Epistles*, VI.16)

THE START OF THE ERUPTION – 1 PM, 24 AUGUST AD 79

Pliny the Younger's vivid account brings the horror of the volcanic eruption to life for us. Now scientists have joined historians in trying to piece together the sequence of events that destroyed Pompeii, Herculaneum and other towns along the coastline. In the early afternoon of 24 August 79 AD, Pliny the Younger's mother had drawn the attention of his uncle, Pliny the Elder, to a large cloud rising up in the shape of a tree. They were looking at molten ash and pumice being ejected from the crater at almost the speed of sound (1000 kph/620 mph). The amount of ash and pumice being emitted was incredible, about 10,000 tonnes (22,000,000 lb) every second, equivalent to 300 juggernauts. Some of this material, the white pumice, started to fall on the area to the south of the volcano. The larger pieces were as big as a small melon. Pumice pieces with a diameter of 1.5 centimetres (0.6 inches) or greater fell at the rate of one fragment per second in every square metre. Overall 10 centimetres (4 inches) of pumice was accumulating on the ground and roofs of Pompeii. The town was bombarded with the pumice for the next 19 hours.

Minutes after the eruption, the column of material had climbed 15 kilometres (9 miles) into the sky and was visible 30 kilometres (18 miles) away, across the bay in Misenum where the Roman navy was based.

The pumice was less dense than water and so it floated in the sea. Mixed in with it, however, were lithics, volcanic rock fragments, dense chunks of dark grey rock torn from the inside of the volcano by the pressure of the erupting magma. These landed with great force, breaking through tiles, smashing windows, and causing serious injury to any people trying to escape.

Opposite above The coastal regions around Pompeii and Herculaneum were dotted with large numbers of sumptuous Roman villas, but escape from the eruption by sea was impossible because of the floating pumice.

Opposite below Eruption damage to the houses is even apparent today. This house has nothing surviving above eaves level; the roof has collapsed inwards due to the weight of ash.

Nothing landed on Herculaneum at this stage; usually at this time of year the wind blows from the north-east, which would have taken the falling volcanic material out over the sea and Herculaneum. But the wind blew from the north-west, taking the fallout directly over Pompeii. The people of Herculaneum had a clear view of the volcano, but the grey eruption column was poised almost directly above them, and they felt the continuous tremors of the volcano as it shook walls and brought down buildings still under repair following the earthquake of a few years before.

THE ERUPTION CONTINUES – EARLY AFTERNOON, 24 AUGUST AD 79

By 2.30 pm the sky above Pompeii darkened as if it were dusk, obscured by the grey eruption cloud and the volume of ash and falling pumice. To the south and west a line of light could be seen on the horizon, just like sunrise or sunset, but it was the middle of the day. Over Pompeii people would be lighting lamps, and getting seriously worried. The pumice layers would be building up, roofs creaking and occasionally a large fragment of stone would crash through a roof. By now the buildings were shaking from the constant earth tremors, with furniture and fittings being smashed. There would have been panic all over the city. Millions of tonnes of pumice floated on the sea, and the wind blew it on to the shore, where it would hinder rescue attempts. Pliny the Elder was forced to abandon his rescue mission because his warships could not land on the coast near Pompeii due to the floating pumice and the tonnes of ash falling on them.

Vesuvius was now ejecting magma at an even greater rate, and the column of material over the volcano had grown to 16 kilometres (10 miles). Climbing up into the stratosphere – twice the height at which airliners fly – the millions of volcanic particles rubbing together triggered spectacular lightning strikes. Over 100,000,000 tonnes of material had already been ejected and the streets of Pompeii were 50 centimetres (20 inches) deep in ash and pumice. As the rate of ash fall increased, so did the size of the pumice particles; some had doubled in size and were large enough to be fatal on impact. Ash accumulated at 13 centimetres (5 inches) per hour, the ash was difficult to walk on and making escape problematic for the people.

Although by this time Pliny had reluctantly given up his rescue mission, he continued by boat for Stabiae.

LATE AFTERNOON, 24 AUGUST AD 79

By 5 or 6 pm over 50 centimetres (20 inches) of pumice stone had accumulated on the roofs of Pompeii. Roofs would have been collapsing all over the town from the weight of the material on them. The ash column had risen steadily to 27 kilometres (16 miles) and the volcano was throwing out an astonishing 40,000 tonnes of ash per second, which was spreading inexorably over a much larger area. Although the winds were carrying the ash away from Herculaneum, the cloud of debris over Vesuvius had a slight mushroom shape, so as it was lifted higher, the leading edge of the mushroom ended up right over Herculaneum. Herculaneum itself was now being shaken by constant earth tremors; in the Villa of the Papyri, just outside the town, archaeologists have found large pieces of wall plaster on the floor where they had fallen as a result of the building being shaken. The vibration would have been continuous, with rumbling and occasional larger shocks. Serious damage would have been caused to buildings as the roofs caved in. The people of Herculaneum would have tried to escape, with crowds congregating on the beach, waiting for rescue.

During this time, Pliny was sailing towards the home of his friend Pomponianus at Stabiae. He arrived there in the evening and then bathed and dined.

DARKNESS – 7.30–8 PM, 24 AUGUST AD 79

Opposite In the eighteenth century Sir William Hamilton painted Vesuvius erupting and threatening the neighbouring town of Naples.

By the evening the pressure of the eruption would have opened up the volcano's cone. A staggering 100,000 tonnes of material were now being ejected every second. It reached 30 kilometres (18 miles) into the sky – almost three and half times the height of Everest.

The eruption pattern changed: the magma was now coming from much deeper inside the chamber. It was hotter, heavier, and not so rich in gas. As the column became denser it also became less stable and more likely to collapse. For the inhabitants of Pompeii this was their last chance to escape.

At Herculaneum, people saw a red jet rising from the summit of the volcano, it was almost 3 kilometres (2 miles) high, but the dark billowing clouds of ash obscured most of it. The ash cloud also had a lot of lightning, some of the flashes extending to the height of the cloud. People in

Herculaneum would have seen this amazing light show and, at the same time, tremors through the ground would have made everything vibrate.

OVERNIGHT TERROR –
1–2 AM, 25 AUGUST AD 79

At around 1 am the first of six pyroclastic surges occurred. The people of Herculaneum had been watching the eruption for hours, and very little ash had fallen on them, but the optimistic were not unduly concerned. Suddenly, they would have noticed that something different was happening. A huge glowing red fountain shape emerged from the column of ash and cascaded down the sides of the volcano. The volcano's mouth had collapsed and the amount of material being ejected increased to 150,000 tonnes per second. The ash cloud had reached its peak, 33 kilometres (20 miles) above the crater. The column was now so dense that it did not mix properly with the air carrying it upwards and it began to collapse.

The glowing red cloud flowed down the slope of the volcano towards Herculaneum. This avalanche of dry, hot ash, rock fragments and gas travelled at a speed of 100 kph (62 mph) with a temperature in excess of 815°C (1500°F). Suddenly the billowing, glowing, hot, dry, surge cloud

rushed down the streets of Herculaneum. It spilt over the city walls and buildings like dry ice. In three to four minutes the surge had overrun the town. It swept over buildings, up the surrounding hills and across the sea. The surge was impossible for people to outrun and those sheltering in the boatsheds stood no chance. There were a handful of people on the beach, who were killed within seconds – those inside the boatsheds died instantaneously, as the surge rushed into the small, confined spaces. There was no escape; everybody was killed.

The people on the beach died of thermal shock. At such high temperatures, their skin vaporised and their bones were incinerated. Their brains

Death, the great leveller. Nobody survived, young and old, wealthy and poor, huddled together awaiting rescue that never came.

boiled, then exploded. Even today, their skulls are still stained from the red cerebral matter that poured out. Like glass that shatters under boiling water, their bones snapped in half and their teeth disintegrated.

Archaeologists have found over 250 bodies on the beach at Herculaneum. The surge had collapsed, leaving behind a relatively thin layer of ash, just a few centimetres deep in most places. Bodies were not completely buried. Minutes later, the surge was followed by a pyroclastic flow of heavier material – volcanic fragments, ash, pumice, tiles, bricks and masonry, and bits of wood that destroyed the remains of the buildings and buried everybody and everything in just a few seconds. Inhabitants of the nearby town of Oplontis would have suffered the same fate, but they may not have even seen the surge coming.

At 2 am the second pyroclastic surge overran the small town of Terzigno and again Herculaneum and Oplontis. The people of Terzigno would have been killed with little warning, like those at Oplontis, for the ash fall was so thick they too might not have even seen the surge.

At Stabiae, Pliny the Younger described the heavy ash fall and the strong earthquakes: 'By this time the courtyard giving access to his [Pliny the Elder's] room was full of ashes mixed with pumice-stones, so that its level had risen, and if he had stayed in the room any longer he would never have got out... They debated whether to stay indoors or take their chance in the open, for the buildings were now shaking with violent shocks, and seemed to be swaying to and fro as if they were torn from their foundations.'

The people of Herculaneum were already dead after the first surge, but with the second surge the city had started to disappear, and by sunrise it would be buried under 25 metres (82 feet) of debris.

A FINAL WARNING FOR POMPEII – 6.30–7 AM, 25 AUGUST AD 79

The third surge at 6.30–7 am reached the north wall of Pompeii. It was still very dark, even though the sun had risen the only light was a glimmer on the horizon under the ash cloud to the west. With visibility so poor, few would have seen the surge coming. They would have heard it, however, and felt its burning 400°C (750°F) heat. Those outside would have fallen victim to the choking, foul cloud of gases that followed. It quickly spread

Above All that is left of a once-prosperous city is the bare brick bones of the buildings. Vesuvius, looming behind, buried the city, but much damage was also done by pillagers over the centuries.

Left The decomposed bodies of the victims left hollow spaces in the ash which Giuseppe Fiorelli, in 1884, began to fill with liquid plaster. This solidified and exactly reproduced the shape of the body.

throughout Pompeii. Carbon dioxide, evil-smelling hydrogen sulphide, hydrogen chloride and sulphur dioxide, the gas cloud put the weakest out of their misery.

Although by this time it was daylight elsewhere, in Stabiae Pliny the Elder was still in darkness 'blacker and denser than any ordinary night'. Misenum had not been badly affected until dawn, when Pliny the Younger noted 'the light was still dim and faint', and the earthquakes were so severe that 'the buildings around us were already tottering'. It was the earthquakes that finally made Pliny the Younger decide to leave. By the time he left his house the streets were full of people also trying to flee the city.

THE END OF POMPEII – 7.30–7.45 AM, 25 AUGUST AD 79

The eruption column had reduced in height to 16 kilometres (10 miles) after the third surge. Although after 15 hours the volcanic eruption was running out of steam, something triggered another surge which this time headed straight for Pompeii. The eruption column collapsed with a pyroclastic surge far bigger than before. Travelling at 100 kph (62 mph), the fourth surge took only a few minutes to reach the town. Hot ash blasted in through chinks in doors and windows, holes in roofs. It killed most of the remaining inhabitants of Pompeii, but death was not instantaneous. With the first breath, hot gas and ash were inhaled, causing the lungs to fill with fluid: it was like swallowing fire. The second breath took in more ash, which mixed with the fluid to create a wet cement in the lungs and wind-pipe. The third inhalation thickened the cement, causing the victims to gasp for breath – and suffocate. Because death was slightly slower than in the Herculanean boatsheds, people writhed in agony on the ground, unable to breathe, which accounts for the contorted positions of some of the bodies.

The surge was cooler than at Herculaneum, causing the slower deaths, but it was hot enough to carbonise any dry organic material, including wood, curtains, clothes, trees, and bushes. All of Pompeii was on fire, with its inhabitants lying in the death throes of an unimaginable disaster and covered in a thin shroud of fine ash. The fifth surge came a few minutes later, covering much the same area as surge four and further terrorising the people fleeing the earlier surge.

Opposite Pompeii was doomed but there was no escape, even to the mountains. The sixth surge at 8 am reached many kilometres south of the town killing everything in its path. It was the end of Pompeii and the surrounding districts.

ARMAGEDDON – 8 AM, 25 AUGUST AD 79

Within minutes, the fate that had befallen Pompeii was visited on the whole of the Bay of Naples. After almost 24 hours of continuous eruption, Vesuvius delivered its final blow. A sudden increase of material ejected into the unstable column set off the collapse of the whole lower half, which spread lethally in all directions.

The sixth surge at 8 am was enormous. It reached many kilometres further than the previous flows, particularly to the south of the volcano, and probably killed everyone who fled Pompeii in the early morning following the fourth and fifth surges. The surge went right across the Bay of Naples in both directions, the edge of the cloud just reaching Pliny the Younger in Misenum and Pliny the Elder in Stabiae. There 'the flames and smell of sulphur', which gave warning of the approaching fire, drove the others to take flight and roused Pliny the Elder to stand up. He stood leaning on two slaves and then suddenly collapsed: 'I assume that his breathing was impeded by the dense fumes, which blocked his windpipe – for it was constitutionally weak and narrow, and often inflamed.' The surge cloud devastated Campania, killing many thousands who had fled into the countryside around Vesuvius.

Pliny the Younger survived the tragedy to give the only eye-witness account of the sixth surge in a letter to Tacitus written 20 years later:

> You tell me that the letter in which, at your request, I described the death of my uncle has made you want to know what fears and even what dangers I myself experienced, having been left behind at Misenum (in fact, I had reached this point when I interrupted myself). Although I tremble at the very memory, I will begin.
>
> After my uncle's departure, I gave the rest of the day to study – the object which had kept me at home. Afterwards I bathed, dined and retired to short and broken sleep. For several days we had experienced earth shocks, which hardly alarmed us, as they are frequent in Campania. But that night they became so violent that it seemed the world was not only being shaken, but turned upside down. My mother rushed to my bedroom – I was just rising, as I intended to wake her if she was asleep. We sat down in the courtyard of the house, which separated it by a short distance from the sea...

...Though it was the first hour of the day, the light appeared to us still faint and uncertain. And though we were in an open place, it was narrow, and the buildings around us were so unsettled that the collapse of walls seemed a certainty. We decided to get out of town to escape this menace. The panic-stricken crowds followed us, in response to that instinct of fear, which causes people to follow where others lead. In a long close tide they harassed and jostled us. When we were clear of the houses, we stopped, as we encountered fresh prodigies and terrors. Though our carts were on level ground, they were tossed about in every direction, and even when weighted with stones could not be kept steady. The sea appeared to have shrunk, as if withdrawn by the tremors of the earth. In any event, the shore had widened, and many sea-creatures were beached on the sand. In the other direction loomed a horrible black cloud ripped by sudden bursts of fire, writhing snakelike and revealing sudden flashes larger than lightning.

My uncle's friend from Spain began to argue with great energy and urgency. 'If your uncle is alive, he would want you to be saved; if he has perished, he would have wanted you to survive. Why, then, do you delay your escape?' We replied that we could not think of our own safety before finding out what had happened to him. Without a moment's further delay, he left us abruptly and escaped the danger in a frantic headlong rush. Soon after, the cloud began to descend upon the earth and cover the sea. It had already surrounded and obscured Capreae [Capri], and blotted out Cape Misenum. My mother now began to beg, urge and command me to escape as best I could. A young man could do it; she, burdened with age and corpulence, would die easy if only she had not caused my death. I replied that I would not be saved without her. Taking her hand, I hurried her along. She complied reluctantly, and not without self-reproach for hindering me.

And now came the ashes, but at first sparsely. I turned around. Behind us, an ominous thick smoke, spreading over the earth like a flood, followed us. 'Let's go into the fields while we can still see the way,' I told my mother – for I was afraid that we might be crushed by the mob on the road in the midst of the darkness. We had scarcely agreed when we were enveloped in night – not a moonless night or one dimmed by cloud, but the darkness of a sealed room without lights. To be heard were only the shrill cries of women, the wailing of children, the shouting of men. Some were calling to their parents, others to their children, and others to their wives – knowing one another only by voice. Some wept for themselves, others for their relations. There were those who, in their very fear of death, invoked it. Many lifted up their hands to the gods, but a great number believed there were no gods, and that this was to be the world's last, eternal night. Some added to the real danger with false or illusory terrors: 'In Misenum,' they would say, 'such and such a building has collapsed, and some other is in flames.' This might not be true, but it was believed.

A curious brightness revealed itself to us not as daylight but as approaching fire, but it stopped some distance from us. Once more, darkness and ashes, thick and heavy. From time to time we had to get up and shake them off for fear of being actually buried and crushed under their weight. I can boast that, in so great a danger, I did not utter a single word or a single lamentation that could have been construed as weakness. I believed that one and all of us would perish – a wretched but strong consolation in my dying. But the darkness lightened, and then like smoke

A mother and child caught in the death throes of suffocation. Fiorelli's method of preserving these figures allows us to relive such scenes of terror.

or cloud dissolved away. Finally a genuine daylight came; the sun shone, but pallidly, as in an eclipse. And then, before our terror-stricken gaze, everything appeared changed – covered by a thick layer of ashes like an abundant snowfall.

We returned to Misenum, where we refreshed ourselves as best we could. We passed an anxious night between hope and fear – though chiefly the latter, for the earthquakes continued, and some pessimistic people were giving a ghoulish turn to their own and their neighbours' calamities by horrifying predictions. Even so, my mother and I – despite the danger we had experienced and the danger that still threatened – had no thought of leaving until we should receive some word of my uncle.

Such were the events; and you will read about them without the slightest intention of including the information in your works, as they are unworthy of history... Adieu! (*Epistles*, VI. 20)

AFTERMATH

Preservation can be extraordinary in its random choice. Whilst grand buildings were utterly destroyed, eggs packed in clay have survived.

Herculaneum lay buried under 25 metres (82 feet) of volcanic material, Pompeii under some 4 metres (13 feet). When the flows were moving they would be full of extremely hot gas and air and would have been greatly inflated to several metres deep. When it settled, however, it was only about a metre deep. The later surges were much denser. The eruption produced 9 billion tonnes of material. In addition, other ash added a further 1 billion tonnes to the erupted material. The ash fall was traced as far away as Egypt and North Africa. Mud rain started falling after the final surge at 8 am. After a while the rain would cause flooding in the the form of mud (lahars). It took several hours for the ash to clear in the atmosphere. 'At last the darkness thinned and dispersed into smoke or cloud; then there was genuine daylight, and the sun actually shone out, but yellowish as it is during an eclipse' (Pliny the Younger).

Everything was grey because of the ash and familiar landmarks had disappeared. Herculaneum was

Over two thousand people died in Pompeii alone, thousands more in the other towns and surrounding countryside. Each year many more bodies are found by farmers and builders still buried where they fell.

completely buried. The shoreline had moved out by several hundred metres and the area was unrecognisable. Pompeii was buried to a lesser degree; the surges had demolished most of the upper stories of the various structures, but some of the tallest buildings and gates were probably still visible.

The amount of material that was randomly preserved by the blanket of volcanic lapilli covering Pompeii and Herculaneum was quite extraordinary. When archaeologists discovered the Temple of Isis, fresh eggs and fish were still laid out on its dining-room table. In the kitchen of the House of the Vettii, pots still stood on the kitchen tripods and contained meat bones. In the bakery of Modestus 81 loaves were still in the oven. In the *macellum*, the market building in Pompeii's forum, there was fruit in the glass containers.

At Herculaneum, the preservation is as amazing. On the dining-room table in the House of the Relief of Telephus, lunch had been set out – bread, cakes and fruit. In the shop of the Drinking Priapus, three large jars of nuts were preserved under the counter with a few set out in dishes on the counter.

Vesuvius has erupted many times since Pompeii was buried, most recently in 1944. Never again, however, has it unleashed the same annihilating, apocalyptic force as on that bright August day in AD 79.

UNCOVERING THE LOST CITIES

After the eruption of Vesuvius in AD 79, little of Pompeii and Herculaneum remained visible above a layer of volcanic material. The Emperor Titus quickly arranged for a commission of senators to be appointed to look after the interests of the devastated area. Survivors had fled to Nola, Neapolis (Naples) and Surrentum (Sorrento). The property and land of families who had been wiped out in the disaster were sold, and the money used as a relief fund for the survivors. The undamaged fields belonging to Pompeii were given to the community of Nola and the survivors of Herculaneum settled in Neapolis.

Opposite **Probably belonging to Quintus Poppeus (who was related to Poppaea, wife of the Emperor Nero), the House of Menander is one of the most important in Pompeii. After the eruption thieves tunnelled into the complex, but were trapped by falling masonry. The thieves were later found by modern archaeologists, still clutching their spades and lanterns.**

An exquisite cameo glass vase found in a tomb outside the Herculaneum Gate. Reputed to have still contained wine when found, it is decorated with cupids harvesting grapes and playing music.

The commission of senators was instructed to plan the rebuilding of Pompeii and Herculaneum, but the damage was too great, too many had died. It was left to Stabiae, on the edge of the disaster area with access to the sea, to take over the maritime trade of Pompeii. However, rescue parties got to work almost straight away. At Pompeii, gangs of military personnel used the roofs of buildings still standing above the debris as a guide to where to dig. The rescue parties left graffiti on walls exposed by tunnelling. The messages read: 'Broken into'; 'There were 50 of them, still lying where they had been'. After the frantic attempts to rescue survivors in the first few days, attention was probably diverted to the valuable building materials and imperial statues in the forum. Although there is some discussion about when the statues, paving slabs and marble facings were removed, it seems likely to have been after the eruption of Vesuvius in AD 79 rather than as a result of the earthquake some 15 years earlier.

The location of Pompeii and Herculaneum was, with time, forgotten. The people of Campania even forgot the name of Pompeii, referring to the hill that covered it as '*la civita*', the city.

THE FIRST EXCAVATIONS

In 1594 Count Muzio Tuttavilla employed the architect Domenico Fontana to dig an underground tunnel to divert the waters of the River Sarno to power grain mills at Torre Annunziata. The workmen uncovered Roman walls decorated with colourful paintings. Later, in 1689, some inscriptions were found, one referred to a Pompeii town councillor (*decurio Pompeiis*), initally it was thought this was a Roman villa, unaware that it was actually the remains of Pompeii itself.

At Herculaneum the memory of the buried Roman town had not been entirely forgotten. It had been mentioned in a sixteenth-century book, but buildings were not found until 1706. After a particularly dreadful eruption of Vesuvius that badly damaged the town of Resina, new water supplies were quickly needed. Numerous wells were dug to look for water and one of them, situated in the wood of the Frati Alcontarini monastery, landed on top of the highly decorated stage wall (*scaena*) of the theatre. The Austrian Prince d'Elbeuf, who was building a luxury villa for himself nearby, ordered the well to be enlarged and other tunnels dug off it. The haul, in Roman statues, rare marble and bronze fittings, was fantastic; d'Elbeuf spent seven years, from 1709 to 1716, removing the marble facings and a large group of statues from the *scaena*.

The first real attempts to search for the lost cities began when Charles of Bourbon, King of the Two Sicilies, later to become King of Spain, commissioned a Spanish army engineer, Colonel Roque de Alcubierre, to search for the sites. His instructions from Charles were to supply the Spanish court with statues. What he found was more startling; it was the buried city of Herculaneum.

From 1 October 1738, he enlarged the earlier tunnels into galleries in the theatre area and began new tunnels in all directions. The exploration of the theatre was completed; several possible temples were found, as was the forum and probably the basilica. Alcubierre was aided by the Swiss architect Karl Weber, who had a more systematic approach to the excavations. Daily and weekly reports were issued, unfortunately with few plans, and no record was kept of where objects were found. Alcubierre had problems working with Weber because Alcubierre was after precious objects; he was not interested in recording or even preserving the town. His parties of local diggers, called the *cavamonti*, burrowed through walls decorated with paintings, hacked through mosaics, cut through doors, all to find valuable objects. Weber wanted to record, draw plans and excavate in a more

Many paintings from Pompeii and Herculaneum were removed and sold. The walls of a whole room from the villa belonging to P. Fannius Synistor at Boscoreale, near Pompeii, now reside in the Metropolitan Museum, New York.

Johann Joachim
Winckelmann (1717–68)
wrote *History of Ancient
Art* and helped spread the
appreciation of classical
art throughout Europe.

considered manner. He had his chance when the sumptuous Villa of the Papyri was found buried just outside the town of Herculaneum. Weber spent years in tunnels, exploring and recording the edifice, until 1765 when the tunnels were sealed because lethal carbonic gas began to filter into them. All the tunnels of Herculaneum were left, filled with rubbish and became dangerous, so the site was abandoned. It was left in such an unstable condition that the ground fell in and the villa disappeared from view. Fortunately Karl Weber had made a detailed plan, which revealed that the villa was originally an atrium-style luxury villa. Later it incorporated an extensive peristyle with gardens and pools, and a belvedere at the end of a promenade overlooking the sea. Weber's plan of the Villa of the Papyri is the only plan to have survived of these early excavations at Herculaneum and it is so good that the complex has been replicated in California by J. Paul Getty.

RECOVERING THE ART AND ANTIQUITIES

Johann Joachim Winckelmann was a contemporary expert on ancient art, who had gone to Rome in 1757 to study the antiquities, and in 1762 wrote about the new discoveries at Herculaneum:

> The direction of this work was given to a Spanish engineer, called Roch Joachim Alcubierre, who had followed his majesty to Naples, and is now colonel and chief of the body of engineers at Naples. This man, who (to use the Italian proverb) knew as much of antiquities as the moon does of lobsters, has been, through his want of capacity, the occasion of many antiquities being lost. A single fact will prove it. The workmen having discovered a large public inscription (to what buildings it belonged, I cannot say) in letters of bronze two palms high; he ordered these letters to be torn from the wall, without first taking a copy of them, and thrown pell-mell into a basket; and then presented them, in that condition, to the King. They were afterwards exposed for many years in the curiosity cabinet, where everyone was at liberty to put them together as he pleased. Some imagined they made these two words, IMP. AUG. ...The works in question were committed to a Swiss officer called Karl Weber, now a

major; and it is to his good sense that we are indebted for all the good steps since taken to bring to light this treasure of antiquities. The first thing he did was to make an exact map of all the subterraneous galleries and the buildings they led to. This map he rendered still more intelligible with a minute historical account of the whole discovery. The ancient city of Herculaneum is to be seen in it as if freed from all the rubbish with which it is actually encumbered. The inside of the buildings, the most private rooms and the gardens, as well as the particular spots where everything taken out of them was found, appear in this map just as they would if they were laid quite bare. But nobody is permitted to see those drawings. (J.J. Winckelmann, *A Critical Account of the Situation and Destruction... of Herculaneum, Pompeii and Stabia*, 1771)

Interior of the basilica, the most important building in Pompeii. It was here where all Pompeii met to conduct business, sign legal contracts and listen to court cases.

The Villa of the Papyri was abandoned and it was not until the late 1980s that modern archaeologists decided to re-open the old tunnels. The villa is one of the most sumptuous yet found, situated on a rectangular plateau

just above the Bay of Naples. On the beach below was a small dock. The main house is surrounded by gardens, terraces, walkways, pools and fountains. Weber and his excavators retrieved over 90 pieces of sculpture, the largest collection ever found. They included 11 statues portraying sirens, satyrs and fauns found in the entrance hall. Another large basin of a fountain had 13 bronze panthers spurting water from their mouths. The inner peristyle garden housed a statue of the 'The Spear Bearer', a copy of the famous fifth-century-BC Greek statue by Polyclitus; the first-century-BC copy was made by Apollonius of Athens. Outside, the main garden has wondrous views of the Bay of Naples and in its centre is a walkway lined with 65 columns. The gardens abounded with statues: bronze deer, Greek women, wrestlers, Pan the 'Drunken Faun' and 'Hermes Resting'.

Scattered over the floor of one of the rooms, however, were papyrus scrolls and wax tablets. This may well be the real treasure of the villa, for hidden away in a small room were row upon row of shelves stacked with thousands of books. The problem was how to read them; they were badly scorched and very fragile. In 1753 Father Antonio Piaggio, a specialist in old manuscripts, arrived from Rome. He looked at the disastrous attempts made to unravel the tightly wound scrolls, and built a special machine to unwind the brittle books. It took four years to achieve the unrolling of just three books. By the mid-nineteenth century some 341 had been unrolled with 195 deciphered and published. Recently the Scandinavian classicist Professor Knut Kleve developed a new system of reading ancient manuscripts using digital technology. These remastered works can now be read by scholars, many of whom believe that this technological development is the most important advance in the archaeological world for decades. It is thought that the papyri might include lost works of Aristotle, scientific works by Archimedes, mathematical treatises by Euclid, philosophical work by Epicurus, the lost sections of Virgil's 'Juvenilia', comedies by Terence, tragedies by Seneca and works by the Roman poets Ennius, Accius, Catullus, Gallus, Macer and Varus. Work started on the decipherment of some of the uncovered books under the supervision of Professor Marcello Gigante of the University of Naples. Initial results suggest Calpurnius Piso, the father-in-law of Julius Caesar, owned the villa, as some of the books were written by Philodemus, Virgil's teacher and in-house philosopher of Piso. Work has recently stopped and the programme is now at risk, although the recent threat of flooding to the rest of the buried villa and library now seems to be over. Much of the villa still remains to be discovered and further books, statuary, jewels and paintings are awaiting recovery.

Most of the objects recovered by Alcubierre and Weber are now lost, sold, or scattered around the world in private collections or public museums. However, at the time Charles III created a museum for the artefacts in one wing of the royal palace at Portici. He realised that the finds were important and forbade anyone from trading or possessing archaeological artefacts. He also tried to ensure that all images of the finds were controlled by the State, so much so that a contemporary engraver and writer, Count de Caylus, who was fascinated by the discoveries and visited the museum wrote:

Found in 1895, at the bottom of a wine barrel in the Roman villa at Boscoreale, was a complete set of Roman silver tableware comprising highly decorated cups, platters, drinking vessels, dishes and ewers.

> All the works of art found in Herculaneum are displayed in the exhibition rooms that his majesty the King of Sicily had built at Portici. Those entrusted with the protection of this collection, will not allow a single note to be taken there, and nothing can escape their vigilance. The only remedy, therefore, is to remember at leisure the most important things you noticed. This you may judge for yourselves by my brief account of the entire collection of antiquities to be found in the museum at Portici.
>
> About 700 fragments of paintings, 350 statues, including portrait busts of varying quality, made of either bronze or marble, 700 different vases of various shapes and sizes, almost all bronze, about 20 bronze tripods, around 40 chandeliers of the same metal, 800 manuscripts and 600 other smaller items, such as lamps, instruments, rings, bracelets, necklaces, mirrors, etc. The number of life-size statues amounts to about 40, of which approximately half are in bronze and the rest marble. Vases made of bronze have been unearthed in large quantities, and in general they reveal excellent workmanship and attractive forms, but are always tasteful. In some cases there are foliage motifs, inlaid with silver, encircling the rim or neck of the vase, in others pretty little intertwining figures form the handles, most take the form of jugs, bowls or saucers.
> (*Pompeii and Herculaneum: An Inventory*, 1762)

IDENTIFYING AND UNCOVERING THE LOST CITIES

Charles III had also instructed Alcubierre to investigate Pompeii. Alcubierre visited Fontana's water channel at Pompeii and realised the buildings uncovered were part of a much larger site. Work officially began on 30 March 1748, about 200 metres (655 feet) from the Temple of Fortuna Augusta, close to the Via Stabiana. Alcubierre was too involved with work at Herculaneum to give Pompeii much attention, however. Work only resumed there in 1754 and on 20 August 1763 he uncovered an inscription that referred to 'the commonwealth of the Pompeiians' (*Respublica Pompeianorum*). The lost cities of Pompeii and Herculaneum had now both been found and identified after centuries buried. Work continued on both sites but stopped in Herculaneum in 1765, not to start again for another 60 years. Digging at Herculaneum had been difficult and dangerous; it had been buried up to 20 metres (82 feet) in volcanic material that had set like rock. Digging there meant tunnelling down and then spreading outwards in galleries. At Pompeii only about 5.70-7 metres (19–20 feet) of volcanic material covered the town, so it was far easier to dig and even to clear complete houses. The excavation progressed with the Spaniard Francesco la Vega, who replaced Weber in 1764 and later took control of the site after Alcubierre. La Vega's approach was more systematic, with a general plan of Herculaneum being drawn up for posterity. The contemporary commentator Johann Joachim Winckelmann was somewhat critical of the approach of the excavators, however: 'The works for that purpose are carried on in a very slow and indolent manner, there being but fifty men, including the Algerian and Tunisian slaves, employed in all these subterranean places. Great a City as Pompeii is known to have been, I, in my last journey found but eight men at work on the ruins of it.' (*A Critical Account of the Situation and Destruction... of Herculaneum, Pompeii and Stabia*, 1771)

La Vega discovered the small theatre (*odeion*) and also the Temple of Isis, rebuilt after the earthquake of AD 62 by Popidius Celsinus. The gladiators' barracks were excavated in Pompeii between 1766 and 1795. The Villa of Diomedes was unearthed in 1771; in 1772 18 bodies were found clasped together in an underground room. One of the bodies was of a young girl, which so moved the French novelist Théophile Gautier that he wrote a novel about her – *Arria Marcella* (1852). The finds created a sensation in art and archaeological circles. In 1775 the Herculaneum Academy was founded

The Temple of Isis was discovered in 1765 and painted by Sir WIlliam Hamilton, English ambassador to the court of Naples.

and the Academicians began to produce their publications, including the discoveries from the Villa of the Papyri. The lost cities of Vesuvius became an important stop on the Grand Tour made by all fashionable English and American aristocrats. It provided an impetus to the neo-classical revival, with potters such as Wedgwood producing Pompeii-style dinner services. Robert Adam used stucco motifs from Pompeii and Herculaneum to decorate the interiors of country houses throughout Britain, and Chippendale produced sets of furniture inspired by the classical motifs unearthed.

The news of the discoveries at Pompeii spread: 'It is work which should employ three thousand men,' remarked the Emperor Joseph of Austria. The German writer Johann Wolfgang von Goethe, visiting in 1787, wrote:

> Pompeii surprises everyone by its compactness and its smallness of scale. The streets are narrow, though straight and provided with pavements, the houses small and windowless – their only light comes from their entrances and open arcades – and even the public buildings, the bench tomb at the town gate, the temple and a villa hereby look more like architectural models or dolls' houses than real buildings. But their rooms, passages and arcades are gaily painted. The walls have plain surfaces with richly detailed frescoes painted on them, most of which have now deteriorated. (*Italian Journey*, 1786–8)

In January 1799 the French army led by General Championnet occupied Naples and proclaimed the Parthenopean Republic, which lasted just five months. During this time, however, he ordered the resumption of the now-ceased excavations. Under Napoleonic rule, Joseph Bonaparte expanded the excavations at Pompeii by employing soldiers. Joseph's successor, Joachim Murat, succeeded to the throne of Naples in 1808. The work at Pompeii now had a powerful champion, for Murat's wife Caroline, who was also the Emperor Napoleon's sister, took a keen interest in the excavations there. The workforce had expanded to well over 2,000 people, 1,500 of them army sappers. Caroline funded a lot of the work at Pompeii including a plan to expose all of the town walls, which entailed buying up land around the perimeter. She actively promoted the excavations – she was an avid letter writer – and encouraged the publication of the first guidebooks to the city. She also gave the architect Charles François Mazois access to the most recent discoveries. Murat had commissioned Mazois to work on improvement schemes for the city of Naples in 1808. By the following year he began to concentrate on Pompeii. He made about 450 drawings of the town, including romantic views of the exposed monuments, plans of the excavated areas and numerous studies of objects. Mazois used these images to produce the beautiful engravings in his book *The Ruins of Pompeii*. Published between 1824 and 1838, it was one of the earliest records of the site. Mazois wrote of his schedule of work at the site:

The back of a beautiful silver mirror delicately modelled in a plain style, with the image of Bacchus as the central motif.

Here I am, settled in Pompeii once more, where, in spite of the heat, my riches continue to increase, that is my collection of finds continues to grow. I get up very early; at about 9 o'clock the fierce heat of the sun forces me to take a break, so I return to my small room, where I finalise the sketches I have made during the morning... After I have eaten... I set to work again, in my cramped lodging until 5 o'clock, and then out in the windy open air until sunset.

All in all, that means a total of thirteen or fourteen hours' work a day.
(*The Ruins of Pompeii*, 1824–38)

The objects discovered at Pompeii and Herculaneum had been housed in the royal palace at Portici, which is between Naples and Herculaneum. In 1790 the decision was taken to remodel a large building in Naples, which has now become the National Archaeological Museum. The objects from Pompeii and Herculaneum were placed in the newly converted museum and in 1822 the displays were open for viewing by the public.

The years immediately following the fall of the French First Empire led to a dramatic decrease in the workforce at Pompeii. With just 13 staff, the leaders of the excavations, Antonio Bonnucci and Michele Arditi (director of the museum at Portici) cleared the city of the accumulated piles of excavated earth. In 1823 the forum had been cleared, also the theatre area and the rest of the gladiators' barracks. The area around the Herculaneum Gate, most of the Street of Tombs, the amphitheatre and parts of the Via Stabiana were all successfully cleared. In 1824 excavation was completed at the Forum Baths and most of the Temple of Fortuna Augusta.

From 1825 to 1830 Francis I, King of the Two Sicilies, took immense interest in the excavations of Pompeii. It is said that he liked to take moonlight strolls amongst the ruins. Houses to the north of the Forum Baths, and the House of the Tragic Poets were uncovered during his reign. In 1828 Francis I ordered work to re-start at Herculaneum after an interlude of almost 60 years. This time the tunnels were ignored and larger areas of excavation begun. The work was hard and slow with no tangible results. The ancient town of Herculaneum was so deeply buried under the modern town of Resina that thousands of tonnes of volcanic material had to be dug out before the first buildings were visible. Finds were rare, the work slow and expensive; eventually the King lost interest and digging stopped in 1835.

Francis I's successor, Ferdinand II, continued the excavation work at Pompeii with startling results. In excavating the House of the Faun, his workers discovered a huge mosaic depicting Alexander the Great and Darius at the Battle of Issus, or possibly Gaugamela. The quality of the mosaic work was excellent and the find created tremendous excitement. (It can now be seen in the National Archaeological Museum in Naples along-

Right The battle between Alexander the Great and Darius portrayed in one of the finest mosaics yet to be found at Pompeii.

Opposite Darius and the Persians fleeing from the Greeks. Detail of the Alexander mosaic, from the House of the Faun, Pompeii.

side several fine mosaics from Pompeii and other cities in Campania.) Finds like the Alexander mosaic brought large numbers of travellers to view Pompeii. Some, like Charles Dickens, wrote down their impressions:

> Stand at the bottom of the great market place of Pompeii, and look up the silent streets, through the ruined temples of Jupiter and Isis, over the broken houses with their inmost sanctuaries open to the day, away to Mount Vesuvius, bright and snowy in the peaceful distance; and lose all count of time, and heed of other things, in the strange and melancholy sensation of seeing the Destroyed and the Destroyer making this quiet picture in the sun. Then ramble on, and see, at every turn, the little familiar tokens of human habitation and everyday pursuits; the chafing of the bucket-rope in the stone rim of the exhausted well; the track of carriage-wheels in the pavement of the street; the marks of drinking vessels on the stone counter of the wine-shop; the amphorae in private cellars, stored away so many hundred years ago, and undisturbed to this hour –all rendering the solitude and deadly lonesomeness of the place, ten thousand times more solemn. (*Pictures from Italy*, 1845)

Mark Twain visited the Campania coast on board *Quaker City*, the first cruise liner, and wrote: 'And so I turned away and went through shop after shop and store after store, far down the long street of the merchants,

Tucked into a back street is one of the 30 brothels found in Pompeii. This brothel was built over two floors, with clients reaching the top floor via an outside staircase.

and called for the wares of Rome and the East, but the tradesmen were gone, the marts were silent, and nothing was left but the broken jars all set in cement of cinder and ashes' (*The Innocents Abroad*, 1875). Queen Victoria visited in 1838 and Prince Ludwig of Bavaria was a constant visitor, eventually building a replica Pompeii house (the House of the Dioscuri) at Aschaffenburg.

In 1848 revolution swept Italy and work at the sites was only re-established on a stable basis in 1860, with the unification of the separate Italian states into a new nation. The king of the unified Italy, Victor Emmanuel II, realised how prestigious the excavations at Pompeii were and appointed Giuseppe Fiorelli to lead the work in December 1860. Fiorelli was already well known as an excellent young numismatist. He adopted a scientific approach to the excavations, and worked to a plan he had already drawn that divided Pompeii into nine regions and about 120 *insulae*, or zones of streets, allocating each house with an identifying number. His system is still in use today. Indeed, the numbering system used in this book to identify buildings follows Fiorelli's plan. The first, Roman, numeral specifies the region, the second, Arabic, numeral identifies the insula, and the final Arabic numeral gives the house number. Unlike earlier excavations, which consisted of little more than treasure hunts to fill the palaces and museums of Europe, Fiorelli kept a written record of the work and prepared plans of every building uncovered. Before Fiorelli, excavation reports consist merely of lists of valuable finds. To stop buildings collapsing into the already cleared roads Fiorelli excavated from the roof down, removing all the debris from the site as he went. He made little effort to repair or restore the excavated buildings, his intention being to leave new finds in place, whether wall frescoes or floor mosaics. However, some items were still being removed to the Naples Museum, such as the bronze statues and magnificent wall paintings of the House of the Lyre-Player.

As well as his systematic division and numbering of the site, Fiorelli made another great breakthrough. In 1863 he noted that cavities that resembled bodies were appearing in the volcanic debris material. He invented a method of forcing a special solution of plaster into the cavities, under pressure. The results were spectacular. Fiorelli found that the volcanic ash had solidified around the bodies of both humans and animals, and moulded itself to even the smallest detail. The beggar outside the Nucerian Gate, still carrying his sack of alms, was wearing a pair of good quality sandals, presumably a gift from a benefactor. In other examples the weave and style of clothing are perfectly preserved. Some bodies seem to be covered in layers of heavy outdoor clothing, no doubt put on as protection against the burning, falling debris. Many victims died in agony: the torment of death on their faces is shockingly clear. Even dogs have been found writhing in pain and terror as death overtook them. The technique of infilling gaps with plaster was also used successfully on doors, shutters

This historic photograph shows the excavation and restoration of a *thermopolium* in Via dell'Abbondanza by Spinazzola (1911–23).

and even furniture. This style of investigation helped identify the *lupanar* (brothel), the House of Caecilius Jucundus (V.1.26 in Fiorelli's numbering) and a bakery. In 1860 about one-third of Pompeii had been excavated and Fiorelli wanted to finish excavating the entire town. Despite a workforce of 500 to 700 men, however, this task was not completed when he left for a new post in Rome in 1875. His work at Pompeii continued in the hands of Michele Ruggiero, an architect who had worked with Fiorelli. Ruggiero extended the excavation area eastwards towards the Nolan Gate. He found the Central Baths and the House of the Centenary (IX.8.3), named to commemorate the 18th centenary of the eruption. *Insulae* 4, 5, 6, 7 and 8 were also excavated, as was Region V and the *insulae* 1, 2, 3 and 4 on the Via Stabiana. In the 1880s the cemeteries outside the Nucerian and Stabian Gates were discovered. The culmination of Ruggiero's work was the consolidation and restoration of hundreds of frescoes in the houses exposed by excavation. In particular the House of the Silver Wedding (V.2), named in honour of the silver wedding of the King and Queen of Italy, and the House of the Balcony (VII.12.28).

Giulio de Petra, a well-known epigraphist, became director of the excavations in 1893 and continued the work of his predecessors up to 1901. The highlight of De Petra's leadership was the discovery and excavation of the House of the Vettii (VI.15.1) with the famous painting of Priapus, the god of fertility, in the entrance. The god is portrayed with an outsized phallus placed on one pan of a set of scales and a moneybag on the other pan as a counterweight. De Petra also excavated the House of Lucretius Fronto (V.4.10) in 1900. Excavation work continued in Regions V and VI, situated in the northern part of Pompeii. Additional towers along the city wall were excavated and the Temple of Venus Pompeiana, the tutelary goddess of the city, located and excavated. The temple stands on a promontory overlooking the south-western slopes of the city. Built by Lucius Cornelius Sulla as a statement of Romanisation in 80 BC, the temple, clad in white marble, must have been one of the finest buildings in Pompeii. Investigations were also made of the Temple of Jupiter and the Temple of Apollo. A small part of the Villa of Mysteries was excavated in 1909–10: the rest of this vast 90-room villa was excavated and restored in 1929–30. Its importance lies in the significant cycle of Dionysian paintings decorating all four walls of the dining room (*triclinium*). It seems to illustrate the initiation of a female into the cult of Dionysus.

The *lupanar*, or brothel. The cubicle, with its stone bed, is painted white. Above the doorway are painted 'specialities' of the house whilst graffitti from grateful clients adorn the walls.

TWENTIETH-CENTURY EXCAVATIONS

From 1901 to 1905 the historian Ettore Pais worked on Regions V and VI and finished the excavations of the areas of housing adjoining the Via di Nola and Via Stabiana. Pais also excavated the area around the Vesuvian Gate, exposing the *castellum aquae*, or water tower. The water tower was built on top of the city walls next to the Vesuvian Gate at the highest point in the city. The tower was fed by water from the springs of Acquaro near Serino, which was brought to Pompeii by a branch of the aqueduct that supplied the Roman naval base in Misenum. Inside the water tower there are three outlets that served different parts of the city.

In 1904 Sir Charles Walston proposed recommencing excavation work at Herculaneum. After much energetic canvassing in various academic institutions by Sir Charles, it was decided that the work proposed at Herculaneum was too difficult and dangerous and resources should be, for the time being, focused on Pompeii.

The next director at Pompeii, Antonio Sogliano (1905–10), concentrated on restoration work, perfecting techniques of restoration that are still in use today. He worked on the House of the Silver Wedding (V.2), which was originally excavated in 1893 by Ruggiero. Sogliano also restored the peristyle of the House of the Golden Cupids (VI.17.7). The Cupids (*Amorini*) that gave the house its modern name were found engraved in the bedroom and marble oscilla were hung like windchimes between the columns of the peristyle. Sogliano's other achievements include the restoration and replacement of the balcony of the brothel (*lupanar*). August Mau, a German archaeologist, worked alongside Antonio Sogliano (1905–10) and was responsible for perfecting a wide range of conservation measures which are still used today.

Vittorio Spinazzola (director 1910–24) built on the technical achievements of Sogliano, but decided to stop excavation in the northern regions of the city and concentrate on the southern parts. Spinazzola proposed linking the city centre with the amphitheatre by following the Via dell' Abbondanza. His concern was not to make spectacular discoveries of objects, but to concentrate on revealing more of the commercial centre of the city by focusing on one of its main roads. Unfortunately, the plan was flawed. Spinazzola found that the weight of the volcanic debris and damp soil pressed down on the excavated façades of the buildings, threatening to collapse them into the street. He changed his tactics and whenever he came across a significant building he would excavate the building back to the rear alley. In this way spectacular buildings were excavated that added immeasurably to our knowledge of Pompeii. Spinazzola discovered the House of Paquius Proculus (I.7.1), the House of Lucius Ceius Secundus (I.6.15), the House of the Cryptoporticus (I.6.2), the House of Trebius Valens (III.2.1), the House of the Moralist (V.1.18) and the House of Loreius Tiburtinus (II.5.2). Spinazzola had excavated horizontally, carefully recording the facades and shops of *insulae* 8 and 9 in Region I. He wanted to reconstruct the upper floors with their windows, balconies and roofs as genuinely as possible, and he will always be associated with the excavation of the Via dell'Abbondanza and its fine façades and frontages.

Amedeo Maiuri (director 1924–61) was one of the most important figures associated with Pompeii. He became superintendent on 1 September 1924 and held the post for 38 years. His excavations are remembered by the excellence of the work and his scientific approach to recording. With his appointment the process of excavation was accelerated at Pompeii and work began again at Herculaneum in 1927. The Italian writer Guido Piovene describes Maiuri:

The life-size marble statue of Sabina Poppaea, who married the Emperor Nero in AD 62, the same year that her properties in Pompeii and Oplontis were damaged by earthquakes.

A little below average height, with one shoulder slightly lower than the other, Maiuri, this prince among archaeologists, seems to watch you out of the corner of his eye; obliquely, he envelops you in the gaze of his bright eyes, which, though they can sometimes be hard and piercing, are almost always gentle, with an extraordinary mobility of expression... Maiuri walks with small steps, but he walks for hours at a stretch as seems to be taught in the great school of archaeology. An archaeologist is not just an office worker, but also a lover of the open air. And he has the knack – which, I am sad to say, seems to be dying out – of not imposing on you the great weight of his erudition, but only saying what he knows will be of interest to his interlocutor. In sum, he is one of the great lords of this lordly city, happy to welcome visitors to the site of the excavations and to do the honours. (*Travels in Italy*, 1958)

Maiuri started work on the south side of the Via dell'Abbondanza, concentrating on Regions I and II. He wanted to 'give a vision of one of the most interesting quarters of the town'. His most important work was at the House of the Menander (I.10.4). One of the largest houses in Pompeii, it covered an area of more than 1,800 square metres (19,375 square feet). Probably belonging to the Poppaei family, one of whom, Poppaea, was married to Nero, it is now named after the discovery of a portrait of the Greek poet Menander in one of the wall recesses of the peristyle. Formerly, the building was well known as the House of the Silver Treasure after a large collection of silverware was found in 1930. The treasure comprised 118 silver objects and a hoard of coins. It was found by a ten-year-old boy who had tunnelled into an underground room, and there the treasure was, individually wrapped in canvas and arranged in sets inside a massive ironbound chest. The highlights of the collection are seven pairs of drinking cups with figured pastoral scenes executed with tremendous skill. Some of the silverware may have been made locally, but other pieces show Hellenistic influence of the kind found in Alexandria and coastal cities of Asia Minor.

Maiuri also cleared the amphitheatre and the gymnasium (*palaestra*) next door before completing the outstanding work needed on the Villa of the Mysteries. He tackled the digging of a vast ditch, some 8 metres (26 feet) wide, around the entire circumference of the city wall – a distance of about 3 kilometres (1³/₄ miles). This allowed him to study the building sequence of the walls and to rebuild a number of the fortified towers, including Tower X next to the Vesuvian Gate. Insula 8 was excavated from 1936 to 1941, and the excavation of *insulae* 6, 7 and 10 in Region I was also finished. Maiuri then concentrated his workforce on the southern area of the city between the Via delle Scuole and the Triangular Forum. His intention was to clear away the volcanic debris from the terraces. In doing so he revealed one of the most unusual features of Pompeii. The houses were found to be terraced, with wonderful views over the surrounding countryside and sea. Maiuri repeatedly remarked that an understanding of the history of Pompeii would come only from digging deeper than the Roman levels.

He decided to do just that in the most significant areas of the town. He focused on the forum, the temples, the oldest houses and the city walls. Maiuri excavated for a number of years in these areas and he discovered the pre-Samnite city wall that confirmed the Greek influence in the city after the Battle of Cumae (474–450 BC). Investigations of the Doric temple in the Triangular Forum cast new light on the area in the Greek and Samnite occupation. Maiuri also found sufficient evidence to prove there was an Etruscan influence during the period the temple was operating, and there were earlier houses dating back to the Samnite period underneath the Roman houses. He was determined that what was discovered should stay *in situ* and not be removed to museums. However, recently there has been criticism of his methods. It has been suggested that most of the areas he excavated were restored in a makeshift manner and then practically abandoned. Although the most recently excavated, the areas excavated by Maiuri have deteriorated the most. By now about three-fifths of Pompeii had

been excavated along with a much smaller area at Herculaneum.

In 1940 Mussolini entertained Bernhard Rust, the German Minister of Education, in the Roman dining room of the House of Menander. Work stopped during the Second World War, but the allies, believing German troops were hiding in the ruins, bombed repeatedly during August and September 1943. Over 160 bombs were dropped on Pompeii, causing untold damage and shaking the surviving buildings to their very foundations. The bombing badly damaged the Houses of the Faun (VI.12.2–5) and the Moralist (IX.4.1–3) and the museum (Antiquarium). However, when the bomb debris was cleared away from the museum, the Villa of the Marine Gate, with its magnificent paintings in the dining room, was found underneath. Bombing also caused damage outside the city walls in the suburb of St Abbondio, but again, once the debris had been cleared away, the remains of

The House of Menander is named after the painting of the comic poet Menander, painted onto the wall of the central niche opposite the peristyle.

a Temple of Dionysus dating back to the pre-Roman era were revealed. In a stroke of good fortune, however, 60 cases full of valuable objects from the excavations that had been stored in the monastery of Monte Cassino were removed only days before it was destroyed by allied bombing.

POST-WAR WORKS

In 1951 work started again on the site as part of a public works programme. Construction companies provided workmen who removed the volcanic material to be used in the construction of the motorway from Naples to Salerno. Excavations commenced once more in Region I and, with hundreds of workers on site, the area was completely cleared in ten years. The speed of excavation was alarming. For instance, the House of Ceres (I.9.13) was excavated in 12 weeks. Gardens and open spaces were fully excavated, often leaving the smaller rooms and enclosed spaces still filled with volcanic material for future excavation.

Although Maiuri had stated on a number of occasions that the project represented 'a complex, laborious, arduous, slow and costly work of preservation, protection and restoration', the results of recent research on his work show that most of the records are poor and largely unpublished. However, over 500,000 cubic metres (17 million cubic feet) of earth and volcanic debris had been removed from around the city wall between the Marine Gate and the theatre complex. In addition the city wall was revealed in all its grandeur, along with the wonderful houses of Region VIII, whose large picture windows, patios and terraces had given the Pompeians superb views of the Sarno Valley and beyond to the Bay of Naples.

Maiuri retired in 1962, after 37 years as the director of excavation at Pompeii and Herculaneum. He was succeeded by A. De Franciscis (1961–76), who concentrated on restoration work rather than uncovering the site. The only excavation he undertook in Pompeii was of the

A banqueting scene from the *triclinium* of the House of the Chaste Lovers. Painted in the third style, it portrays two couples reclining on couches during dinner. The house is named after the couple kissing tenderly.

wonderful House of Polybius (IX.13.1–3), named after Caius Julius Polybius, whose name was found scratched alongside the household shrine (*lararium*). F. Zevi (1977–82) and G. Cerulli Irelli (1982–4) started to repair the damage done to Pompeii by the earthquake of 1980. As superintendent of Pompeii from 1984, B. Conticello began a complete restoration of all the exposed buildings starting with the *insulae* in Regions I and II; he also began the excavation of the House of the Chaste Lovers (IX.12.6), named after a painting with a banqueting scene in which a couple seem to be kissing affectionately. P. G. Guzzo took over as superintendent in 1994 and concentrated on planning for the future. It had been decided that large-scale excavation would stop and the funding available would be spent on restoration and small-scale excavation to understand better the historical development of the town.

The peristyle of the House of the Chaste Lovers undergoing excavation. Modern excavation is able to provide details of the plants grown in what was once a wonderful garden.

Although 44 hectares (108 acres) of land have been excavated over the last two centuries, the 22 hectares (54 acres) remaining at Pompeii, mainly in Regions I, III, IV, V and IX, are to be left unexcavated for future generations of archaeologists, with more time, expertise and funding. The achievement of archaeologists to the present day has been profound. The excavated towns of Pompeii and Herculaneum have given us an insight into an ancient world that came to an abrupt and violent end around 1 pm on 24 August AD 79.

THE PUBLIC BUILDINGS

Since the 1970s the practice of archaeology and the investigation of sites have changed beyond recognition. Earlier investigators were primarily concerned with retrieving works of art. Impressive examples of architecture were recognised as such, and efforts made to preserve them. Nowadays, archaeological techniques are so refined that an army of specialists is required. Excavations are now hugely expensive, the cost of analysis, recording and preservation of the site even more so. In addition, at major tourist attractions, such as Pompeii and Herculaneum, there is a demand to reconstruct the buildings in their original glory.

Opposite Panoramic view of the interior of the amphitheatre. Built in 70 BC, it is the earliest such building used for gladiatorial games found in the Roman world.

Pompeii was a fortifiied city throughout its life. Here, the city walls, including the tower in the foreground and the Herculaneum gate in the background, survived the eruption of AD 79 and still stand today.

The focus of archaeological work at Pompeii and Herculaneum in the last few decades has been on recording and publication. Some excavation has been undertaken by following in the footsteps of Maiuri and investigating the archaeology below the AD 79 levels, to obtain a further understanding of the pre-Roman town. The future of Pompeii, with its millions of visitors, is in preservation and consolidation, however. Already far too much has been lost, stolen or destroyed. At Herculaneum, the temptation to excavate even more wonderful buildings should be resisted and the focus, as at Pompeii, must be on preservation. The work done over the centuries has exposed about 60 per cent of Pompeii. This has given modern archaeologists the opportunity to study and try to understand the town itself.

TOWNSCAPE

The town of Pompeii covers an area of about 66 hectares (163 acres) enclosed in a defensive stone wall of some 3 kilometres (1³/₄ miles) in length. The shape of the town is an irregular oval, with the terrain inside the walls sloping from a height of 40 to 10 metres (130 to 33 feet) above sea level. The highest part of the town is to the north-west, in Region VI.

The ground slopes down to the south-east where there is a steep drop on to the edge of the ancient lava flow on which Pompeii is built. This gradual slope is bisected by a deep depression running north to south, which was later utilised by the town planners as a road, now called the Via Stabiana. Two small hills were built on at a very early date; the Temple of Apollo occupied the one to the west, and the Temple of Hercules and Minerva the hill to the south. The temples precede the establishment of the town. A market place, which eventually became the forum, grew up in the flat area between the two temples and probably served both. Regular blocks of urban housing called *insulae* were built around the market place and the Via Stabiana. Four separate areas seem to have been developed: the forum, the *insulae* fronting the Via Stabiana, Region VI and the eastern area. The forum area and the *insulae* along the Via Stabiana seem to be earlier than the two other areas, which may have been planned incorporating the geometric principles of the Greek architect and urban planner Hippodamus of Miletus. Hippodamus planned Thurii in the south east of

A view from the Vesuvius gate over the ancient city of Pompeii to the modern city beyond.

The main street in Pompeii, a view down the Via dell'Abbondanza towards the amphitheatre. Note the stepping stones across the street and the public water fountain just beyond.

Italy in about 443 BC. The principles of town planning derived from this town filtered through Italy into Campania, where Capua was renowned for its layout. At Pompeii some of Hippodamus's principles seem to have been forgotten. The grid is not as precise as in other planned towns, but Pompeii does represent one of the earliest known planned cities in Italy.

THE ROADS

Two main roads cross Roman Pompeii – the Via Stabiana and the Via dell'Abbondanza. These are, of course, the modern Italian names. In most cases the Roman names for the roads are unknown, although it is possible that the Via Stabiana could have been named the 'Via Pompeiana' the Latin translation of the Oscan inscription found at one of the gates. The internal road of importance is the Via di Nola that runs westwards from the Nola Gate. At Herculaneum the roads are narrow, averaging about 3 metres (9 feet) wide, the narrowest 2.5 metres (8 feet) and the widest 7 metres (22 feet), providing good protection from the sun. At Pompeii the roads are much wider. At night the streets would have been illuminated by torches; one electoral advertisement found in Pompeii mentions a lamp lighter (*lanternarius*).

At Pompeii and Herculaneum raised pavements ran on each side of the road. At the latter the Romans had constructed an efficient drainage and sewage system under the street, but Pompeiians relied on cesspits and excess water ran down the streets. To avoid this pedestrians had to use the stepping-stones that crossed the road at numerous points. The Romans could apparently live with the stench, which to modern noses would probably be intolerable. The road surface was constructed of a grey, hard-wearing Vesuvian lava stone, still used in the construction of the streets of Naples.

Visitors often remark on the deep ruts scored by carts into the thick flagstones of the road and ask; 'How did the Roman carts and wagons negotiate the large stepping-stones?' The axles of the carts were high enough to miss the stones, and the horses or oxen were attached to the carts only by a yoke, allowing the animals a greater freedom of movement from side to side than is common today. Nevertheless some of the stepping-stones were removed in 1815 to accommodate the Queen of Naples' coach when she visited.

THE GATES

At the end of the principal roads are the seven city gates. The Marine Gate is located at the western end of Via dell'Abbondanza; while at the eastern end is the Sarno Gate. The Marine Gate, which allowed access to the harbour, was originally constructed from large blocks of stone (*opus quadratum*) with two arches, one for pedestrians and the other, much larger, for goods traffic. Subsequently, the gate was rebuilt in mortar and stone (*opus caementicium*). The Sarno Gate, 1,080 metres (3,550 feet) from the Marine Gate, consisted of a single archway giving access to the countryside near the River Sarno. It is the least well-preserved gate, having been robbed of its stone, but enough remains to suggest that it was originally built during the Samnite period.

The Via Stabiana, running north to south along the steep prehistoric lava slope is the main street (*cardo maximus*) of Pompeii. It links the Vesuvius Gate in the north and the Stabian Gate in the south – both single gateways. The Vesuvius Gate was badly damaged by the earthquake of AD 62 and was still under repair in AD 79. Next to the gate stands the water tower (*castellum aquae*) and outside it there is a group of tombs, including that of the *aedilis* Vestorius Priscus, which has fine paintings in its interior.

Entering the city through the Nuceria Gate, the crowds for the amphitheatre beyond would have been controlled by the police stationed at the gates.

The Stabian Gate, built of limestone blocks (*opus quadratum*), is one of the earlier city gates; only the arch and parapet are Roman. Inside the archway can be found an Oscan road-building inscription, whilst outside another inscription in Latin records that the road was paved by the *duumviri* L. Avianius and O. Spedius. Again, as in the case of the Vesuvius Gate, there are tombs immediately outside it. One is the tomb of Marcus Tullius, the benefactor of the Temple of Fortuna Augusta (see p.50) The roadway is deeply rutted at this point, indicating heavy traffic from the port.

At the end of the upper east-west axis the roads Via della Fortuna and the Via di Nola ended at the Nola Gate to the east, and the Via Consolare, running slightly north-west, ended at the Herculaneum Gate to the west. The Nola Gate, built in the late third century BC, has a single tall archway with the keystone of the arch on the city side decorated with a carving of the head of Minerva, the Roman goddess of crafts and trade guilds. The Herculaneum Gate, with its three arches, is one of the most impressive in the city. Called the *porta saliniensis* in the Roman period, it led to the salt-pans where seawater was evaporated in shallow pools to make salt. The present structure dates from the Roman period and is not defensive in construction, but it sits on the foundations of an earlier fortified gate. The gate is constructed of small blocks of stone alternating with bands of brick. The core is mortar and crushed stone; however, most of this stone and brickwork would have been covered in plaster. The Herculaneum Gate leads to one of the most important extramural cemeteries alongside the road to Herculaneum and Naples.

The Nocera Gate served the Via di Nocera. Its impressive height indicates that the original steep access road may have been cut away over time by wear and tear. This gate, with the adjacent Sarno Gate, provided access to the games and the amphitheatre for crowds from the surrounding districts.

THE WALLS

Running between the gates of Pompeii were the city walls, the earliest in earthwork and palisade. By the sixth century BC a low wall built of stone (*pappamonte*) was added, followed by a double curtain-wall built of square blocks of Sarno stone. A single wall with a ditch and bank (*vallum* and *agger*) later replaced this. A walkway was constructed on top of the wall protected by a crenellated parapet until it was finally constructed in its present form. Twelve towers were probably built before 100 BC, spaced at irregular intervals, most in the northern sector, where the ground is flat and more vulnerable to attack. Although Vitruvius, the Roman architect and engineer, wrote that round towers are less prone to damage than square towers, the towers at Pompeii are quadrangular and built on three levels. The first level was built into the body of the walls, the second was the same height as the raised walkway, and the third was a viewing and fighting platform. Access was via a small doorway at the foot of the tower, or an external staircase to the middle level. All 12 towers were self-sufficient, containing food stores, water tanks and barracks for soldiers so they could fight on even if the city had fallen. Indeed there are six inscriptions, written in Oscan, giving instructions to the soldiers manning the walls. The inscriptions are painted in large red letters at various locations in the city. They are known as the '*eituns*' and apart from the directions to the troops, they give valuable topographic information on the city: 'For the next crossing the detached soldiers must go between tower XII and the Salt Gate, where Maraius Atrius son of Vibius is commander.' These inscriptions confirm there were 12 towers and that the Herculaneum Gate was originally called the 'Salt Gate'.

After the conquest of Pompeii in 89 BC by Sulla, the towers and walls lost their importance, although two towers, II and III on the southern side, can still be seen intact in the contemporary painting of the amphitheatre riot in AD 59. Large stretches of wall were demolished to make way for houses on either side of the Marine Gate and it seems that many proprietors illegally built over the public land of the *pomerium*. Vespasian (AD 69–79) sent Suedius Clemens, his envoy, to enforce the law. Although some buildings on the inside of the walls were removed, the sumptuous houses overlooking the Sarno Valley were not.

WATER SUPPLY

Pompeii sits on a high, hard, dry plateau of prehistoric volcanic lava. In the early years of the settlement the only water supply would have been from the River Sarno, wells or the water storage tanks (*impluvia*) built under the floors of the houses. The water-table at Pompeii is about 20 metres (65 feet) under the surface. Wells were dug for both public and private use. The public wells were situated in the Via Consolare at the corner with Vico di Narciso, in Via del Foro and in the forum and Stabian Baths. There were also wells by the Triangular Forum and the Vesuvius Gate, and in the south-east corner of the basilica. Archaeologists have also discovered a number of private wells in homes.

An important source of water for Pompeiian households was the rain-water collected off the atrium roofs. The roofs sloped inwards and the rain fell off the roof through the square opening (*compluvium*) and into the central ornamental pool (*impluvium*) where it would overflow into a large storage cistern underneath. The water was then collected with a small bucket dropped through the ubiquitous marble wellhead.

A constant supply of water to Pompeii was available from the early first century AD. The people had the Emperor Augustus to thank for authorising the diversion to Pompeii of part of the water supply for the Roman naval

The crossroads between Via dell'Abbondanza and Via di Stabia. To the left are the remains of a four-sided monumental arch dedicated to the Holconia family, to the right is a tall water tower to facilitate a continuous supply of fresh water to the fountain below.

base at Misenum. The imperial aqueduct branched off at Palma Campania and divided again, one branch going to Naples, the other to Pompeii. The water was received at a water tower (*castellum aquae*) specifically built for the purpose and close to the Vesuvius Gate, the highest point in the city. It was channelled through a series of sluices and settling tanks, and then supplied three pipes at different heights with separate priorities. The first pipe fed a large public fountain built on to the water tower and then these pipes ran a few centimetres under the pavement along the Via di Stabiana and Via dei Vetti, branching off into all areas of the town. The slope built up the water pressure and, to ensure equal pressure throughout Pompeii, 14 secondary towers (*castella secundaria*) were built with a lead tank at the top that could regularise the pressure (*castellum plumbeum*). From these secondary towers, running water was available through pipes on tap to all the fountains, public baths, and private households. It is amazing how much of the population benefited from the availability of this fresh, clean, running water. There were 42 public fountains across the town, all connected to the secondary water towers by lead pipes. Most of these fountains were a standard shape and consisted of large blocks of stone cramped together (pairs of stones pulled together by a bronze or iron clamp). On the side of the basin closest to the pavement there was usually a post decorated by ornate carvings of gargoyles, water deities or animals. The waterspout, usually a bronze pipe, was located in the centre of the carving and connected to the under-pavement lead pipe (*fistula*), typically pear-shaped and sealed with an overlap strip welded along the top. The water ran into a public fountain continuously and overflowed through a drainage hole into the street. Consequently, the water in all the 42 fountains was always clean and abundant.

In the houses of the rich we can see decorative basins (*nymphaea*) and gardens full of fountains and water features. All of Pompeii had access to running water. The earthquake of AD 62 severely damaged the entire system, and although repairs were rapidly completed, it seems that further damage was done to the network of pipes prior to AD 79. This may suggest severe earthquake damage in the years or months leading up to AD 79. Recent archaeological surveys have indicated that there were many deep trenches in pavements still open on the day of the eruption. No doubt they were awaiting repairs to the water system.

A marvel of Roman engineering, this valve enabled the water supply to be regulated from the fourteen water towers dotted around Pompeii.

BUILDING MATERIALS

No good local building stone was available to the craftsmen of Pompeii and Herculaneum. Consequently various types of stone were bought in at different periods and earlier excavators used these to try to date the various phases of construction. In the House of the Faun there are at least five different phases of construction, at the Villa of the Mysteries, six. Until the third century BC the larger houses of Pompeii were constructed from blocks of Sarnus stone, a travertine rather than limestone found in the Sarnus valley. It was pale beige in colour, very porous and quite difficult to work but excellent for building. Grand houses in the late third and early second centuries BC utilised Vesuvius lava stone in their construction. The stone was dark grey, heavy and basaltic in character. Yellow tuff was quarried from the Phlegrean fields, just north of Naples. It was soft, porous and did not weather well. Grey tuff from Nuceria and Samus was less friable, fine-grained, strong and easy to work.

Terracotta bricks were made in different sizes and shapes, and crushed brick mixed with mortar was used in numerous applications. Sarno stone was incorporated into rubblework walls from the third and into the early second century BC. *Opus incertum* incorporating Sarno stone and lava rock was a building technique used in the second century BC, whilst for carving architectural details and ashlar facades Nuceria tuff was the preferred material. *Opus reticulatum* was introduced as a building method after the Roman colony was established in 80 BC. The construction utilised pyramid-shaped blocks of lava, then later Nuceria tuff, laid diagonally in a lattice pattern. The last building technique, *opus listatum* (also known as *opus vittatum mixtum*), most common after the earthquake of AD 62, used brick courses alternated with small blocks of Sarno stone or Nuceria tuff.

After the earthquake a variety of cheap and cheerful building methods came into use. One, *opus craticium*, utilised a crude lattice framework of timber filled in with roughly laid masonry using whatever building materials were to hand. The Trellis House at Herculaneum is a good example of this technique, whilst at Pompeii numerous internal partitions used the same method.

Building construction techniques cannot be used as a precise dating method. The analysis is complicated by the continuing use of the *opus incertum* method throughout the period. There are, however, two other

Wall mosaic at its very best, the delicate polychrome mosaic cubes, some less than a centimetre square, adorn this wonderful fountain in the House of the Scientists.

methods that can aid in dating the various phases of construction. The first is the interior decoration. Houses of the Roman wealthy usually had richly decorated floors and walls. Floor finishes and mosaics, as well as wall paintings, can be used to date construction. The first Pompeiian style of wall painting runs from the second to the early first century BC, the second style from about 80 BC to the last years of the first century BC, and the third from the end of the first century BC to the mid-first century AD. The fourth style emerged during the city's last 30 years. The floor surfaces of the buildings of Pompeii and Herculaneum are less easy to date. Some floor surfaces are *opus signinum*, a waterproof mixture of crushed tile and mortar, others are *lava pesta*, mortar and crushed lava decorated on the surface with spaced marble tesserae. Both can be dated to the second and first centuries BC. Grid patterns of single marble *tesserae* (*punteggiato regolare*) are usually associated with the first style of painting, whilst true mosaics with coloured emblems belong to the first and second style.

'Beware of the dog'; one of Pompeii's most enduring images is to be found in the entrance hall of the House of the Tragic Poet.

True mosaic floors consisted of thousands of small cubes of stone, glass or marble, called *tesserae*. The *tesserae* were laid on a bed of mortar and tamped down with a flat piece of wood to produce a horizontal surface. Once the mortar was dry, the *tesserae* would be grouted with a slurry of mortar in an appropriate colour, cleaned off and then 'waxed' with a coating of olive oil. This sealed the floor, protecting it from staining, and also enhanced the colours of the mosaic. The finest mosaics looked more like eastern carpets than floor tiles. The simplest mosaic style, *opus tessellatum*, usually featured geometrical patterns and was made of larger tesserae. Mosaics with pictorial scenes were made of much smaller *tesserae*, occasionally less than 1 centimetre ($^1/_2$ inch) square; this technique was called *opus vermiculatum* and the pictorial scene, normally in the middle of the mosaic floor, was known as an *emblema*. Black-and-white mosaics appear late in the second style and finally the use of fragments of

coloured marble set into the pavement indicates a date of the late first century BC.

The second method of dating the building of walls, which has been much neglected by archaeologists in the past, is the use of pottery. Modern excavators have proved that most walls and floors, to some degree, contain fragments of pottery that can be dated and therefore give an indication of when the structure was built.

The forum at Pompeii surrounded by a double storey colonnade. To the right are plinths for Imperial equestrian statues whilst at the far end stand the remains of the Temple of Jupiter, framed by two imperial triumphal arches.

THE FORUM

As in all Roman cities, the forum was the heartbeat of the community. It was here that the administrative and legal business of the city was conducted. Magistrates were elected to take part in religious ceremonies under the watchful eye of the emperor. Townspeople met country people in the plazas. There were markets for vegetables, fish, meat, and for the sale and exchange of bulk commodities like grain, cloth and wool. All these activities were controlled, measured and regulated by elected representatives of the people, and are illustrated on the painted frieze (31 metres/101 feet long) found in the House of Julia Felix. It shows a large crowd of shopkeepers, cattle merchants, vegetable sellers, bronze workers, cloth merchants, hauliers and shoemakers thronging around the porticoes of the forum.

The political life of the forum was dominated by the annual elections of the two *duoviri iure dicundo,* the highest legal authority in the city, and the two lesser-ranking *duoviri aediles*. The former were responsible for law and administration and presidency of the Pompeii senate, which was an assembly of local council members, the *ordo decurionum*. The *aediles* were responsible for maintaining the roads, public buildings and temples and for supervising the markets and organising the games. The *duoviri iure dicundo* who held power at the time of the five-yearly elections assumed the title of *quinquennales*. They also had to conduct the census and revise the list of *decuriones*, who had to meet various criteria of wealth, status and so on, and number no more than 100.

The forum we see today dates back to the second century BC. Earlier, in the sixth century BC, it was a market place that grew up at the crossroads close to the Temple of Apollo. With the end of the second Punic War, the population of Pompeii expanded considerably and as trade increased the wealth generated was invested in the monumental rebuilding of the forum. The old market place was rebuilt as an elongated rectangle some 137 metres (450 feet) by 47 metres (156 feet). Two-storey colonnaded porticoes with Doric columns surrounded the south and two long sides. The paving along the edges was of tuff slabs whilst the rest was surfaced in concrete. Later, possibly in the Augustan period, new paving was laid in travertine stone. The paving was incised with large letters filled with lead that gave the name of the magistrate responsible for the work. Very little of this paving survives and might have been salvaged by the Romans immediately after the eruption in AD 79. The most important buildings surrounded the forum, and contemporary illustrations indicate the probable appearance of these buildings. The fourth-style paintings in the atrium of the House of Julia Felix are the most important, because they not only show a fleeting glimpse of everyday life in the forum, but they also depict architectural details. They show porticoes hung with garlands and a number of equestrian statues on plinths arranged around the sides of the forum.

A relief-cut slab from the House of Caecilius Jucundus (V.1.26) portrays the buildings on the north side of the forum during the earthquake of AD 62. The Temple of Jupiter is shown leaning, with statues tumbling from their plinths. The temple, dedicated to the Capitoline triad – Jupiter, Juno and Minerva – was built in the middle of the north side of the forum. Its function, as guardian of all political activity, superseded the ancient Temple of Apollo, which was separated from the forum and given its own space enclosed by a four-sided Hellenistic-style portico. On the opposite side of the forum, the south side, were grouped the buildings housing the political and legal machinery of the city. They included the Hall of the Duumviri, the Curia and the Hall of the Aediles. To the east was the so-called *comitium,* where the town magistrates were elected, and to the west the basilica. The meat and fish market (*macellum*) was located on the east side, and south of it were the Temple of the Public Lares, the Temple of Vespasian and the Building of Eumachia. On the west side of the forum, just to the south of the public latrines, was located the *holitorium* where cereals were sold. Further south on the west side was the *mensa ponderaria,* where weights and measures were checked. The large paved area of the forum was embellished with numerous statues, unfortunately removed either before or immediately after the eruption of AD 79. Along the centre of the western side can be found the platform (*suggestum*) from which election candidates could canvass. Vehicular traffic was banned from the forum, and access for pedestrians and litters, the ubiquitous 'taxis' of Roman towns, was by two monumental staircases leading from the Via Marina or Via dell'Abbondanza.

The forum, in its final stage of development, represents an architectural statement of public space that displays the cultural and economic strength of the community. It is unfortunate the forum was so badly damaged during the earthquake of AD 62 and that by the time of the eruption 17 years later little restoration work had started. The largest structures in the forum, the capitolium and the basilica, had undergone no renovation at all.

THE TEMPLE OF JUPITER

Situated on the north side of the square, the Temple of Jupiter dominates the forum. It is flanked by two triumphal arches: the one on the west side possibly dedicated to Augustus, the other, on the east side, probably dedicated to Germanicus. Both arches were constructed of *opus latericium* and faced with white marble slabs and were surmounted by bronze groups of equestrian statues.

The temple replaced the Temple of Apollo as the epicentre of political and religious life. When the Temple of Jupiter was built as a large tuscanic temple in the second century BC, it measured about 56 feet (17 metres) by 121 feet (36 metres) and it had six Corinthian columns along the front of the building and four along the sides. The *cella* or shrine, which covered three-fifths of the surface of the podium, was used as a base for the statue of the deity, probably Jupiter. The rooms under the podium were used for storing offerings and temple regalia. Archaeologists have found a large altar situated 3 metres (9 feet) in front of the podium.

The building was completely reorganised immediately after 80 BC, when the Roman colonists of Sulla descended on the town. The temple was transformed into a *capitolium* dedicated to the sacred triad of Jupiter, Juno and Minerva. The joint protectors of the Roman state and the most important gods in the Roman pantheon, they were even venerated on the Capitoline Hill in Rome. The podium base inside the *cella* was rebuilt and lengthened to house the three statues, but only two fragments survive: the head of Juno and the torso of Jupiter. The temple had two access staircases built into the podium and a new altar built on the central platform. On either side of the altar were two smaller platforms mounted by equestrian statues. The *cella*'s entrance door led into a large room which was divided into a nave and two aisles by two colonnades. The lower storey is Ionic and the upper storey Corinthian. At the end of the shrine was the podium, which supported the statues of Jupiter, Juno and Minerva. Inside the podium there were three small rooms, found stacked with precious marble sheeting by the excavators. It has been suggested that between the earthquake of AD 62 and the eruption in AD 79, the area was being used as a marble workshop.

The interior of the temple is decorated in the second style with red-painted lower courses (*orthostatae*) which are divided by painted marble pilaster strips framed top and bottom with multicoloured rustication. A painted corbel at the top contains the decorative paintwork. The floor is made of cut marble pieces called *opus sectile*. This example has diamond-shaped pieces laid in a pattern to create the illusion of three-dimensional cubes. This fine pavement is contained in an outer banding of black-and-white mosaic.

THE TEMPLE OF APOLLO

The cult of Apollo was from the start one of the most important in Pompeii. Indeed, the god was worshipped as the town's protector up to the time of Sulla. Located to the west of the main forum, so the temple could be seen from afar, it established the domination of the area by the cult of Apollo very early on. On the shrine floor there is an *omphalos* or 'navel', the symbolic centre of the world, probably referring to the Apollo cult at Delphi. The earliest traces on the site were found by Maiuri when excavating in the 1930s and 1940s, and dates from the end of the seventh century BC. The cult was obviously of Greek origin, there are Greek temples of Apollo at both Cumae and Naples. However, the Etruscans adopted the cult very early on, as seen in the Etruscan Temple of Apollo at Veii. Archaeologists have found Greek and Etruscan pottery in trenches around the site. The earliest temple was much larger, but the entire area was reorganised in the second century BC when the

Standing close to the temple of Apollo is the bronze statue of Apollo portrayed as an archer. Found in fragments, the original is in the National Archaeological Museum of Naples.

forum and most of its associated buildings were erected. The temple still played an important part in the lives of the inhabitants of Pompeii – its portico was connected to the newly built forum by 11 entrances which were blocked only when Sulla's Roman colonists introduced the cult of Jupiter in 80 BC. The religious and political focus was now on the capitolium, or Temple of Jupiter, that dominated the northern end of the forum.

When the Temple of Apollo was first excavated in 1816–17, it was thought to be the Temple of Venus. The discovery of the name of Apollo cut into the pavements and of a bronze statue of the god inside the portico of the temple eventually corrected the identification. The temple is surrounded by a peristyle comprising nine columns on the north and south sides and 17 columns on the east and west sides. The columns were carved from grey Nuceria tuff in the style known as the Composite order with Ionic capitals. The columns were remodelled into the Corinthian order and painted yellow after the earthquake of AD 62, and the capitals were coloured yellow, red and blue.

An altar of Greek marble stands in front of the temple. This was re-dedicated by the four magistrates, the *quattuorviri*, one of whom was Marcus Porcius, who also built the *odeion* theatre and the amphitheatre. The temple has a wide staircase that gives access to the podium. The shrine is surrounded by a peristyle of six columns on the north and south sides and ten on the east and west sides. Inside the shrine, and close to the back wall, stood a pedestal that supported the statue of the deity, but, unfortunately, this was missing when the shrine was excavated by the archaeologists. The floor of the shrine is made of green and white *opus sectile* diamond shapes arranged to look like cubes – similar to the floor surface of the shrine of the Temple of Jupiter. The *opus sectile* floor is banded in slate and an inscription in Oscan on the front band reads: 'Quaestor Oppius Campanus... sponsored the building... by resolution of the council, which was paid for by the offerings to Apollo.' The date of the inscription is the second half of the second century BC.

Outside, and to the west of the temple steps, stands a marble column surmounted by a sundial. Erected in the Augustan period, it is one of about 30 sundials found in public places and private gardens of Pompeii. Close by are a number of statues standing on pedestals, including bronze statues of Apollo and Artemis portrayed as archers. The statue of Apollo was found in several fragments and later reconstructed and a copy placed in the temple. The original is in the National Archaeological Museum of Naples. The statue of Artemis, also found near the temple, is probably from the same workshop.

THE IMPERIAL CULT

The imperial cult effectively presented the emperor as a divine being to the Roman Empire's population. Surviving evidence of the imperial cult in Pompeii is concentrated on the east side of the forum. This includes the public buildings of the Temple of Vespasian, the Temple of the Public Lares and, just outside the forum proper, the Temple of Fortuna Augusta. The imperial cult was also evidenced by shrines in buildings of a commercial character, such as the Building of Eumachia and the *macellum*.

THE TEMPLE OF VESPASIAN

The so-called Temple of Vespasian, just north of the Building of Eumachia, has a façade of *opus latericium* and was probably originally faced with sheets of marble. The entrance that leads through into the temple portico comprises four columns that may have held up a roofed vestibule. The temple area inside is totally enclosed by a high wall, which is pierced by a small door in the south side of the back wall, leading to three rear rooms. The shrine abuts the back (east) wall and has two flights of steps on either side for access to the podium. The magnificent altar in the centre of the unroofed area is faced with four white marble slabs with relief decorations and surmounted by a further white marble slab. The face one sees first on entering the temple shows, in some detail, a sacrifice of a bull. A veiled priest is attended by various individuals, all of whom had a particular role to play in the ceremony. The sacrifice was performed in the open, as all pagan sacrifices were. The ritual was unlike anything practised in the Christian faith. The first requirement was that nobody should be present who would

The Temple of Vespasian is an open space enclosed by a high wall. In the centre is an altar of white marble carved with sacrificial scenes.

contaminate the proceedings. Women, for instance, were excluded from sacrifices to Hercules and Mars. The priest (*popa*) and those who were involved in the sacrifice washed their hands in holy water, after which the herald called for silence: '*favete linguis*' ('Check your tongues'). The flute player then started to play; he was employed to drown out any extraneous noises. The priests covered their heads with the folds of their togas, again to muffle any noises that might intrude on their thoughts, and, taking up a platter heaped with sacred flour mixed with salt (*mola salsa*), sprinkled the mixture between the horns of the animal held firm by the attendants and over the sacrificial knife. The bull then had all its decorations removed while an attendant symbolically drew a knife along its back from head to tail.

It was at this point in the service that the prayer was made. The prayer had to be carefully written and memorised; any mistake at this point invalidated the entire ceremony. The suppliant turned towards the cult-statue within the temple. The climax of the ceremony had now been reached. The *popa*, standing on the right of the animal, asked, '*Agone?*' ('Do I strike?') and, if the suppliant replied 'Yes', struck the animal's head with his hammer. As the stunned animal sank to its knees, the knife-man (*cultrarius*) stepped forward, lifted its head to the gods and slit its throat. Blood spurted everywhere. The moment of death was important; it had to be a clean death without incident. The animal was then dismembered and the internal organs removed for inspection. These had to be perfect, because the inside of the animal was as important as the outside. These organs, called *exta*, were cut into small pieces (*prosecta*) and put on the altar for the gods to consume as the meat was burnt in the flames. The whole procedure was detailed and exact, perfected by generations of tradition. In the hands of skilled priests the ceremony was probably both devout and moving.

On the other faces of the altar in the Temple of Vespasian are the various instruments used in the sacrifice ceremony. The north-facing marble slab shows the long outer garment (*stola*) worn by the priest, the sacrificial rod (*lituus*) and the incense box (*acerra*). The south slab shows the platter (*patera*) to hold the sacred flour and salt, and the ladle (*simpulum*). The east side of the altar, which faces the temple, is decorated with a crown of oak leaves between two laurel branches.

The temple was probably dedicated to the tutelary deity of Augustus. An inscription found at Pompeii reads: 'Mamia, daughter of Publius,

The altar in the centre of the Temple of Vespasian shows, in some detail, the sacrifice of a bull. The veiled figure is the chief priest surrounded by various attendants.

public priestess, on her own land and at her own expense dedicated to the Genius of Augustus.' This inscription is likely to have come from the temple. Certainly all the portrayals on the main altar reflect the cult of Augustus, which dates from 27 BC. The oak-leaf crown was the prerogative of the emperor and was awarded to Augustus by the senate of Rome for bringing peace to the empire. It is likely the temple was originally dedicated to Augustus, and later adapted to the imperial cult of Vespasian. Interestingly, the temple is one of the few to undergo restoration after the earthquake of AD 69. It is likely it was quickly restored so that the townspeople of Pompeii could appeal directly to the emperor for funds to repair the public areas of the town devastated by the earthquake.

THE BUILDING OF EUMACHIA

Next door to the Temple of Vespasian, at the southern end of the east side of the forum, is a large building that has been identified as associated with the guild of fullers (*fullones*), the wool merchants, dyers and launderers. It has been suggested that the building might have been a sort of wholesale wool market, but recent research points to its use as a slave market. What is, however, certain is that the priestess Eumachia built it. Two inscriptions

The city of the dead (Necropolis) situated outside the Nuceria Gate contains the large tomb of Eumachia, chief priestess.

have been found in the building. The one carved on the architrave of the forum portico reads: 'Eumachia, public priestess, had the *chalcidicum*, *crypta* and portico built in her name and that of her son Marcus Numistrius Fronto and dedicated its construction to the harmony and devotion of Augustus.'

The *chalcidicum*, or vestibule, is the area between the colonnade fronting the forum and the front of the main building. It could be closed at either end by metal gates. A saddle roof built of timber trusses covered the *chalcidicum*. The front of the building was faced with white marble and was aligned with the forum and not with the building itself, which is oriented on an axis parallel to the Via dell'Abbondanza situated on the south side of the building. The central entrance has a marble portal decorated in relief with acanthus volutes and fauna. The quality of the work suggests that Roman rather than provincial craftsmen made the carving. Stylistically it is comparable with the quality of work to be found on the Ara Pacis in Rome. On either side of the entrance are niches with inscriptions in praise of Romulus and Aeneas next to large apses, which probably contained statues of the emperor's ancestors.

At the far end of the front wall were two rectangular galleries reached by a staircase. These rostra could have been used by auctioneers to sell the wool, or auction slaves. Behind the front wall are various rooms; those to the north were for storage, and the room to the south contains a low platform with a large terracotta pot built into it. It may have been for collecting urine – passers-by were invited to contribute to it and the collected urine, which was taxed by Vespasian, would be used to bleach cloth.

A four-sided portico, built of white marble columns carved in the Corinthian style, surrounded the large inner courtyard. It is thought the portico may have had two storeys. At the east end there is a large apse. This contained a white marble statue of Livia, wife to Emperor Augustus, on a large pedestal. Livia is represented as a richly decorated deity holding the horn of plenty (*cornucopia*) in her arms. The apse was flanked by two gardens that could have been seen from the windows of the apse and from the two niches at either end. Behind the portico on three sides runs a large covered gallery (*crypta*) with ten windows to illuminate the interior. In the middle of the east side of the *crypta*, behind this apse, is a niche where a life-sized statue of Eumachia was found. It was made of white marble and there are traces of the original polychrome colouring. The inscription on the pedestal reads: 'Dedicated by the fullers to Eumachia, daughter of Lucius.' The fact that the statue of Eumachia stands in a secluded area, but immediately behind the apse containing the statue of the Empress Livia, may suggest that Eumachia presented herself as a local equivalent of the emperor's wife. Eumachia, priestess of Venus and member of a local aristocratic family involved in lucrative trading, had probably modelled her building on the Porticus Liviae in Rome.

THE SANCTUARY OF THE PUBLIC LARES

Immediately to the north of the Temple of Vespasian, and on the east side of the forum, stands the sanctuary of the Public Lares – one of the most unusual and least understood buildings in Pompeii. It was originally thought that it was built after the reign of Augustus, but before the earthquake of AD 62, but recent research now suggests that it was actually built after the earthquake. The building was almost square, incorporating an open

The white marble statue of Eumachia, originally painted, was found in a secluded area of the building behind the statue of Livia, wife of Augustus.

area which was surfaced with a pavement of *opus sectile* – cut marble pieces in a geometric pattern of framed squares and circles. In the centre of the pavement stood an altar.

To enter the building visitors passed between eight columns set on basalt bases. On the back wall is a large apse with a low podium running round the semi-circular side which supported a row of columns with a projecting cornice and architrave. The apse was roofed with a dome, probably coffered. On either side of the apse were two large rectangular niches, each with a pedestal for statues. Theories abound about the function of the building. It was thought that the town Lares or gods were worshipped here, but given that the building was designed to hold statues, perhaps of the emperor, it is possible that the imperial cult, associated with the gods of Pompeii, was the focus of worship. An alternative is that it was Pompeii's Augusteum, in memory of the emperors.

THE TEMPLE OF FORTUNA AUGUSTA

Identified from the inscriptions found at the site, the Temple of Fortuna Augusta is north of the forum at the intersection of the Via del Foro and the Via della Fontana. Archaeologists have found earlier floors under the temple, indicating it was built on a site previously occupied by shops and possibly a house. The temple is Corinthian, sitting on a high podium reached by a single flight of marble steps into which the main altar has been set. Work on the temple began in 2 BC and was completed by AD 3.

An inscription found on the architrave of the temple (and now re-inserted into the apse) honours the founder of the temple: 'Marcus Tullius, son of Marcus, *duumvir* with judicial power three times, *quinquennalis*, and military officer elected by the people, erected the Temple of Fortuna Augusta on his land at his own expense.' Once the temple was built, Tullius would have chosen slaves to staff the College of Priests of Fortuna Augusta, which would have been a private rather than public college. The fact that the cult was originally private may have been why the temple occupied an area outside, but very close to, the public space of the forum. The body of the temple comprised a *cella* or shrine with four Corinthian columns on the façade and three on each side.

The shrine, situated towards the rear of the podium, had a large apse in the rear wall where a raised dais, mounted by two columns, framed the statue of Fortuna. Originally, the statue probably held a rudder and horn of plenty (*cornucopia*). The symbol of the rudder represented the belief that the goddess could steer people's destiny. On each of the side walls there were two rectangular dedicatory niches, which probably once contained statues. Archaeologists excavating the temple in 1922 found two statues close by. One was of a man wearing a toga, initially thought to represent Cicero, the other was of a woman with her face badly damaged. Access to the temple was through iron gates at the front. At the rear, service rooms were built for the College of Priests. The building suf-

fered badly in the earthquake of AD 62 and little repair work was carried out. It may even be that the expensive marble was re-used elsewhere.

In the centre of the *macellum* stood a circular pavilion held up by 12 poles resting on stone bases. The pavilion was built as a shelter for traders cleaning fish in the fountain that once stood here.

THE MACELLUM

The *macellum* was the public fish and meat market, situated on the north-east side of the forum. This location, which dates back to some time in the second century BC, is in keeping with the town planning of the period when such activities were removed from the forum proper and re-established on the periphery.

The area in front of the *macellum* is organised on the same lines as the vestibule (*chalcidicum*) of the Building of Eumachia, but was embellished with at least five pediments on which honorary statues once stood. At least five shops have been identified built into the façade of the building. It has been suggested that these were for the moneychangers. The monumental entrance to the market proper is through a central doorway, which housed two marble pedestals. These may have been for statues or two columns that may have supported an entablature that had been built into the side walls. The large internal area of the market had a portico on all four sides and in the middle of the uncovered market stood a type of circular pavilion called a *tholos* held up by 12 poles resting on stone bases. Inside this structure was a large marble counter for displaying fish with a fountain in the middle to keep them cool; a stone gutter surrounded the cobbled floor of the *tholos* and when the drain was excavated it was found to be full of fish scales and bones. Once the fish was cleaned, it was sold in a room in the south-east corner of the building, where a large marble counter was connected to a small drain in the floor to drain away the water from the fish on display.

The south side of the courtyard was divided into 11 shops. So that the heat of the sun did not decay the foodstuffs on sale, the counters faced north to keep them shaded. There are another 12 shops on the north side of the market which also face north. Archaeologists working here have found the remains of grapes, plums, lentils, chestnuts, figs, wheat and bread, as well as sheep and goat bones.

Bread being sold or distributed from a stall at Pompeii. The loaves are circular and marked into segments with a double cross.

The fourth-style paintings, now unfortunately faded, portrayed poultry, fish and vessels to hold food and wine. There are also scenes from the festivals in honour of Vesta, the goddess who protected millers and bakers, whose products were evidently sold in the market too. There was even room in the market for an area dedicated to the imperial cult. On the eastern side a marble staircase flanked by two podia leads into a room with a small temple (*aedicula*) at the end. It would have housed the statue of an emperor and archaeologists have indeed found part of an arm holding an orb. On the side walls were four niches that contained honorary statues. Excavators found two statues they thought portrayed Marcellus and Octavia, the nephew and sister of Augustus. It is more likely, however, that the two statues portray leading citizens involved in either the running, or restoration of the market.

Next door to the imperial shrine is a large room with an *aedicula* in the south-east corner. It probably held a religious statue since there is a small marble altar in front of it. The room was painted with colonnades with garlands and there were cupids between the columns. It is likely that a religious college used the room for meetings and feasts. Unfortunately, very little has survived today apart from the nineteenth-century descriptions by the excavators. The market was badly damaged in the earthquake of AD 62 and was still undergoing restoration at the time of the eruption in AD 79.

The *macellum* sold meat, fish, vegetables and fruit. this glass bowl shows what was on offer: apples, pears, apricots, pomegranates and black grapes.

THE FORUM HOLITORIUM

Situated in the north-west corner of the forum is a large rectangular building used for selling grain and pulses. The front of the building is divided into eight large openings by nine monumental pillars built of *opus latericium*. The floor was originally laid with *opus signinum* decorated with a colourful array of marble inserts. The *holitorium* was badly damaged in the earthquake of AD 62, and at the time of the volcanic eruption, the roof and internal plasterwork had not been replaced. A few metres away to the south there is a rectangular alcove built into the boundary wall of the Temple of Apollo. This housed the *mensa ponderaria* where the weights and measures used in the various shops and markets of Pompeii were checked by public officials. The weighing tables consisted of two stone counters, one above the other. The lower one is preserved and has nine circular cavities of different capacities equal to a standard measure, each of which have a hole at the bottom to release whatever had been poured into them. The table had been in use since the late second century BC and the measures were labelled in Oscan. In 20 BC, the Emperor Augustus implemented a programme to unify and standardise weights and measures throughout the Roman world, with the consequent abolition of old units of weight. At Pompeii the cavities in the weighing table had to be enlarged to the new Roman measures, and most of the old Oscan measurements were erased. An inscription in Latin carved into the marble counter explains: 'Judges and *duumviri* Aulus Clodius Flaccus, son of Aulus, and Numerius Arcaeus Arellianus Caledus, son of Numerius, had the task of equalising the measurements, as resolved by the decurions.'

To the north of the *forum holitorium* are the public latrines. Entry to the latrines was through a small door situated on the north-west corner of the forum. The door led to an antechamber, and then into the latrines containing the seats and drainage. Rectangular blocks of stone supported a wooden bench carved with holes as toilet seats. On three sides a deep channel ran under the seats supplied with continuous running water. There would also have been washing facilities for cleaning the ubiquitous sponge. A slave waited in the antechamber to help the Roman citizens adjust their dress before leaving.

THE BASILICA

Facing on to the south-west side of the forum, the basilica is orientated on an east-west axis with the façade opening on the east side. It is the most important monumental building in Pompeii and is one of the oldest preserved examples of a basilica in the Roman world. Its function was as a covered forum, where business transactions would take place and courts would meet; it was also the workplace of the town council officials.

The building occupied about 1,480 square metres (16,000 square feet), and was constructed in the last decades of the second century BC. A graffiti inscription in Latin on the basilica contains the names of the two Roman consuls of 78 BC. The building follows the pattern of other basilicas, but the main entrance is on the short side overlooking the forum, rather than on the more usual longer side. There are two small entrances on the longer sides; access was from the Via Marina on the north side and Vicolo di Championnet on the south side. The main entrance was through an unroofed vestibule (*chalcidicum*) to five entrances that were fitted with metal gates. The entrance frontage is magnificent: four Ionic columns frame the façade with the capitals carved in grey tuff. The columns stand on basalt plinths that divide a flight of stairs into four entrances. The inside of the huge hall contains a two-storey, four-sided portico with 28 fluted Ionic columns, each measuring 11 metres (36 feet) high. The side walls have 24 Ionic engaged fluted columns. The structure creates a nave and two aisles, the nave being about twice the width of the aisles. The shafts of the fluted Ionic columns are built in one of the earliest examples of shaped bricks and would have been finished with painted stucco. The 52 columns would most likely have held up a huge single-truss double-pitched roof covered with quite large tiles. The largest of them measure 1.2 × 1 metre (4 × 3 feet) and are stamped with the name Numerius Popidius, a tile-maker and former magistrate.

At the back of the central nave stood the tribunal, with rooms below it for the storage of archives. The tribunal was decorated with a stage-like façade of two levels of Corinthian and Ionic columns. This was obviously the platform for the judges; there are no staircases, so access may have been by a wooden ladder which could be easily removed, thus ensuring the safety of the judges, as we know from the speeches of Cicero how dangerous the reactions of the crowd could be during a trial. In front of the tribunal was a large pedestal for an equestrian statue, possibly of the Emperor Augustus.

Immediately in front and to the right of the basilica are three conjoined buildings, which held all the important civil offices of the town. Maiuri excavated here in the 1950s and proved that the buildings date from the second century BC. He also demonstrated that when the structures were damaged in the earthquake of AD 62 they were rebuilt and extended on to the edge of the forum. The three buildings that made up the municipal offices obviously had different functions, but, unfortunately, it is not

A nineteenth-century drawing of the Forum Baths at Pompeii. Of particular interest are the decorative details, easily seen in the nineteenth century, but now badly damaged by exposure to the elements.

possible to be absolutely sure which was which. The central building was the most important and could be the *curia* where the town senate met, the *tabularium* where the town archives were kept, or the office of the *duumviri* or the two *aediles*. All that can be said with any certainty is that the three buildings as a group housed the administration of the town.

THE COMITIUM

The building just to the east of the municipal offices and situated in the south-east corner of the forum is usually identified as the venue where the town magistrates were elected. The unroofed, almost square building was surrounded by high walls pierced by five entrances on the north and west sides. The earthquake of AD 62 severely damaged the walls, and apparently in an effort to stabilise the structure most of the entrances were blocked up.

The south and east walls were decorated with marble and the floor was paved with marble slabs. Built against the south wall is a rostrum with an access staircase. If the building functioned as a *comitium*, voters would enter the building, show their *tesserula*, a voting artefact, and inscribe their name on a ticket which was placed inside a ballot box.

From the rostrum, the magistrate would announce the count of the vote on the election of the two *duumviri* and the two *aediles*. However, if the building functioned only as a vote-counting house (*diribitorium*) with the main voting activity in the forum or basilica, then the votes would only be counted and announced from the rostrum by the outgoing magistrate.

Pompeii's forum was the very heart of the community and one of the most elegant to be found in Italy. Its grandiose buildings reflected the aspirations and achievements of its citizens, yet when the forum and its buildings suffered wholesale destruction in the earthquake of AD 62, the focus of rebuilding seems to have been instead on buildings for relaxation and entertainment – the public baths and amphitheatre.

PUBLIC BATHS

There are at least five sets of public baths in Pompeii, and two at Hercula-neum – the forum and Suburban Baths.

At Pompeii the Stabian, forum, Central, Amphitheatre and Suburban Baths have all been excavated (although the Amphitheatre Baths were reburied soon after their discovery). All the baths follow, more or less, a standard design and procedure. The bathers would undress in the *apody-terium*, then enter the cold room (*frigidarium*), followed by the warm room (*tepidarium*) to be oiled, moving on to the hot room (*caldarium*) where, after a period of sweating, they would be scraped clean with a curved scraper (*strigilis*) before entering a hot bath (*alveus, piscina calida* or *solium*). Returning to the cold room they would take a cold-water bath (*puteus* or *baptisterium*) before being dried and clothed. In some establishments an additional hot, dry room to induce sweating was included. The Romans called this the *laconicum*, believing the Spartans from Laconia originally used it. There were, of course, numerous variations and additions to the basic design, which evolved throughout the Roman period. The baths themselves were public places. Seneca, writing in the first century AD, recounts his experi-ence of lodging next to a public bath in Rome:

> I'm in the midst of a roaring babel. My lodgings are over the baths! Imagine every possible outcry to shatter your eardrums. When the most athletic bathers swing their dumbbells I can hear them grunt as they strain or pretend to, and hissing and gasping as they expel their breath after holding it... There's a lazy chap happy with a cheap massage: I hear the smack of the hand on his shoulders, the sound varying with whether it strikes flat or cupped. If an umpire comes to keep score at the ball game, counting the toss, it's all up with me! Now add the argumentative noisy pickpocket caught in the act and the sound of the man who loves to hear the sound of his own voice in the bath. After that, the people who jump into the pool with an almighty splash, beside those with raucous voices. You have to imagine the dipilator giving his falsetto shriek to advertise his presence and never silent except when making somebody else scream by plucking hair from his armpits. There's the refreshment man with his wide range of cries, the sausage vendor, the confectioner, the men from the places of refreshment shouting their wares, each with his own vendor's cry.
> (*Moral Letters,* LVI, 1ff)

The central heating used in the baths of Pompeii and Herculaneum is supposed to have been invented in the first century BC by Gaius Sergius Orata (Pliny the Elder, *Natural History,* IX.68). Prior to this, bronze braziers would have been used. These occasionally remained in use, as in the men's *tepidarium* at the Forum Baths of Pompeii. With the introduction of central heating, the floors of the *caldaria* and the *tepidaria* were raised on short columns (*pilae*), usually of brick tiles about 20 centimetres (8 inches) square, called *bessales*. On top of the columns large square tiles (*bipedales*) were laid. The floors were covered with waterproof cement (*opus signinum*) and finished with mosaic paving.

The cavities (hypocausts) under the raised floors were filled with hot air distributed from furnaces. The temperature of the rooms could be raised even higher by channelling the hot air upwards into similar cavities in the walls, and occasionally even into the ceilings by the use of pipes or hollow bricks called box flue tiles (*tubuli*). The surface of these hollow bricks was

The rooms of the Stabian Baths are magnificently decorated with stucco relief. This detail shows a figure framed by a twisted double ribbon design with round shields decorated by cupids.

keyed with a pattern so that they could be stuck to the main wall with mortar and readily plastered over. The improved efficiency of the hypocausts and *tubuli* enabled changes to be made to the design of the baths.

The heat generated by the baths meant that the buildings needed fire-proof ceilings, so the Romans used concrete rather than the more usual timber roof. Bath ceilings were often vaulted or domed to regulate the heat through an opening skylight. The cold room of the Stabian Baths at Pompeii has a dome 6 metres (19 feet) in diameter with a circular opening that dates from the early first century BC. It is possibly the earliest known dome in a Roman building in Italy and a forerunner of the huge arches, domes and apses of the gigantic Imperial Baths of Rome. Vitruvius clarifies the function of the circular opening in these domes:

> The *laconicum* and other sweating baths must adjoin the tepid room, and
> their height to the bottom of the curved dome should be equal to their
> width. Let an aperture be left in the middle of the dome with a bronze
> disc hanging from it by chains. Raising and lowering it can regulate the
> temperature of the sweating bath. The chamber itself ought, as it seems,
> to be circular so that the force of the fire and heat may spread evenly
> from the centre all round the circumference. (*De Architecture,* V.X.5)

THE FORUM BATHS

The Forum Baths at Pompeii were of modest size but located in the central part of insula VII.5, close to the forum, and close to shops and several important private houses. It is thought Sulla's Roman colonists built the baths around 80 BC. The baths were organised into two distinct parts, a male area and smaller female area. Each set of baths had separate entrances so that the sexes could be segregated whilst bathing. The design of the interior was typical of this type. However, these particular baths did have an early *laconicum* modelled on similar baths found in Greek gymnasia. The room was expressly used for a *sudatio*, a hot air bath akin to a modern sauna. The *laconicum* was later re-built into a cold plunge-bath (*frigidarium*), probably because of problems in controlling the temperature.

The male baths could be entered through three separate entrances, two leading to the gymnasium and one to the changing room (*apodyterium*). The gymnasium area had a three-sided portico, with Doric tuff columns on the north and west sides, coated with a thick layer of plaster painted red. The east side had a narrower portico without columns but with arched pillars. Originally, the gymnasium would have been much longer and extended to the north edge of the forum with possibly the main entrance situated here. At some stage the gymnasium's forum frontage was redeveloped and four shops (*thermopolia*) built selling hot and cold food. After bathing, visitors would use the gymnasium to exercise or walk, meet friends or purchase drinks or food.

Visitors paid a small fee at the entrance hall on entering the baths, and left clothes in the adjoining changing room. The room was large and barrel-vaulted; masonry benches ran along the side. There were no niches for clothes, but nail holes in the walls indicate that there was wooden shelving instead. An overhead glazed window set in a metal frame lit the room. The walls of the changing room were painted yellow and the ceiling and end walls (*lunettes*) of the barrel vault decorated with stucco decoration. One of the stucco features is the head of Oceanus, the Greek god of the ocean, with a long, flowing beard and crowned with crab claws. On the south side of the changing room a small doorway led to the circular cold room, which had a large round bath (*balneum*) with four semi-circular niches overlooking it. The bath, covered in marble sheets, was fed cold water from a pipe that can still be seen on the south wall. The drainage and overflow pipes are also still *in situ*. The cupola ceiling had a glazed skylight at the top and was decorated with stucco in a shell pattern. The stucco relief frieze shows cherubs competing in a chariot race. The changing room had a second doorway on the west side that led to the warm room, which served as an acclimatising room before the bather entered the full heat of the next room. The warm room was heated to about 40°C (104°F) – just above body temperature. Here the bather would sweat. It is likely that the bather would be anointed with oil and other unguents kept in the niches of this room.

The conservation of the decoration is excellent, and gives an indication of the splendour of these establishments. The large panels of painted stucco are divided into diamond and rectangular shapes in-filled with mythological figures. The niches, which contained towels and oils, are separated by wonderful terracotta figures (*telamones*), sometimes naked or covered with animal skins, which support the architrave from which the vault springs.

The ceiling of the warm room (*tepidarium*) of the Forum Baths is magnificently decorated with large stucco painted panels divided into diamond and rectangular shapes, infilled with mythological figures.

The floor is well preserved and is of white mosaic surrounded by a black mosaic border. The warm room had no under-floor heating, but was warmed by a large bronze brazier decorated with cows' heads that was donated by Marcus Nigidius Vaccula. Three low bronze benches are also preserved. An entrance through the west wall of the warm room leads to the hot room (*caldarium*).

The hot room is in good condition; it has a barrel vault decorated with spiral fluting in relief stucco that prevented condensation dripping on to the bathers. On the south side is a large apse surmounted by a panel decorated with stucco shells and pierced by a circular window. Situated in the apse (*schola labri*) is a huge monolithic marble basin inscribed on its rim with bronze lettering that read: 'Cnaeus Melissaeus Aper, son of Cnaeus, and Marcus Staius Rufus, son of Marcus, as *duumviri* and judges for the second time, undertook to have the basin built with public money by resolution of the decurions. It cost 5,250 sesterces.' The basin (*labrum*) was provided around AD 3–4. At the north end of the hot room is a large, marble-covered hot-water plunge-bath reached by two steps. The hot room was heated by pipes of hot air in all of the four walls, and under the floors, which maintained a temperature as high at 60°C (140°F). As the floor was heated, it would have been too hot to stand on in bare feet, so bathers wore wooden sandals (*soleae balneares*). The walls were also hot; Fronto wrote: 'As my boys were carrying me as usual from the baths they bumped me a little carelessly against the scorching entrance to the baths. My knee is both grazed and burnt.'

The wall decoration of the hot room is an elegant combination of complementary hues of yellow and purple, whilst the floor is decorated by white mosaic bordered by two black bands. The humidity was kept high; water from the *labrum* would be periodically splashed over the hot surfaces to produce steam. Bathers would also drink the cold water from the basin to aid perspiration and splash the water over their bodies to cool down. It could get very hot, Seneca wrote: 'The temperature that men have recently made fashionable is as great as a conflagration, to such an extent that a slave convicted for a criminal act could be boiled alive. It appears to me that today there is no difference between "the bath is hot" and "the bath is on fire".'

To complete the bathing cycle, the bather would then retrace his steps to the cold room for a plunge in the cold bath. Next door to the *caldarium,* and to the west, was situated the furnace room (*praefurnium*), which separated the men's and women's sections. In the furnace room at the forum Baths there were three cauldrons exactly as described by Vitruvius:

> Three bronze cauldrons are to be set over the furnace, one for hot, another for tepid and the other for cold water, placed in such positions that the amount of water which flows out of the hot water cauldron may be replaced from that for tepid water, and in the same way the cauldron for tepid water may be supplied from that for cold. The arrangements allow the semi-cylinders for the bath basins to be heated from the same furnace. (*De Architecture,* V.X.I)

The women's section, next door to the furnace, was smaller and simpler than the men's and consisted of three rooms: the changing room, the warm room and the hot room that contained a hot plunge-bath and a cold-water basin in the corner of the room.

THE STABIAN BATHS

The largest and oldest public baths in Pompeii are the Stabian Baths, which occupy most of the southern area of insula VII.1. Ruggiero excavated the baths, named after the nearby Stabian Gate, between 1853 and 1858. The buildings that survive today date from the second century BC, but it is likely there were earlier, smaller baths, serving a gymnasium for athletic exercises. When these earlier baths were built there were only small chambers with tubs large enough for one person at a time. During the second century BC, the baths were rebuilt in two separate sections for men and women, but with a shared heating system. Initially these sections were not connected and the use of the gymnasium was reserved exclusively for men. These alterations can be dated by the Oscan inscription on the oldest known sundial from Pompeii, which names the magistrate who rebuilt the baths using money from public fines.

The final stage of development of the baths took place around the middle of the first century BC, no doubt to provide extra bathing amenities for Sulla's incoming Roman colonists. An important inscription from the period records that Caius Uulius and Publius Aninius provided for the construction of several new rooms, such as the hot dry room (*laconicum*), later rebuilt as a cold room, and a room where athletes cleansed themselves (*destrictarium*) with a *strigilis*. The same two magistrates restored the gymnasium and its porticoes. During the late republic the great open-air swimming pool (*natatio*) was also restored.

The main entrance to the baths was from the Via dell'Abbondanza. Two further entrances from the Via di Stabia and Vicolo del Lupanare were still being used at the time of the eruption in AD 79. Other entrances that had been rendered unsafe by the earthquake of AD 62 had been bricked up. The main entrance led into a grand porticoed courtyard with a trapezoid layout, usually used as a gymnasium for athletic exercises. The west side, which did not have a portico, housed the large swimming pool flanked by two rooms that contained further pools for washing feet. In the south-west corner stood a large changing room. The façades of these rooms on the west side were decorated with magnificent multi-coloured stucco reliefs, some of which have survived both eruption and excavation. To the north was located a suite of service rooms, including a public latrine and a large room for indoor ball games (*sphaeristerium*).

The baths were situated on the east side of the courtyard. A large furnace room enclosing the usual three cauldrons for hot, tepid and cold water separated the men's section to the south and the women's to the north. The entrance to the men's bath was located in the south-east corner of the courtyard. Bathers would enter a small office, probably where they paid the entrance fee, and then went into the changing room. Unlike the Forum Baths, the Stabian Baths had niches in which to place clothes on either side of the room. The decoration is magnificent with stucco relief shields, nymphs, cupids and various weapons. A sunray background, in which reliefs of flying deities can be seen, surrounds the shields. Once undressed, the bathers moved into the warm room where there were niches for towels and oils. Unlike at the Forum Baths, there was a large lukewarm pool on the east side of the warm room. Once warmed up, the bathers would move through into the hot room. On the east wall was a large hot bath, and on the opposite short wall the marble basin of cold water. The hot room was heated by under-floor heating and by pipes buried in the walls. After the hot room, bathers would return to the warm room to be dried, oiled and massaged. Then it was into the cold room where bathers took a plunge to clean off the oil and close the pores of the skin. This room, accessible only from the antechamber connected to the changing room, was circular with a large pool in the middle. The walls contained four apses and were painted with garden scenes framed with wooden trellis screens. The domed roof, pierced at the top by a glass skylight, was painted to imitate a starry night sky.

The women's baths are separate from the men's and are located on the north-east side of the complex. The main entrance is situated on the Vocolo del Lupanare, just where the waterwheel drew water up to fill a large tank to feed the baths. This apparatus became redundant when water pipes from the aqueduct were laid. The women had a dual-purpose changing room that contained a cold-water pool built into the west wall. This allowed the area also to be used as a cold room. Once changed, the bathers could move into the warm room and on to the hot room, then back to the changing room and the cold plunge bath.

THE CENTRAL BATHS

A new development after the earthquake of AD 62, the Central Baths were meant to provide the centre of Pompeii with the most up-to-date bathing system. Great care was taken to use the most innovative methods, building was done in brick and separate sections for men and women were abolished. The baths occupied the entire area of an *insula* with shops built into the street frontages on the west and north sides. The rooms were larger, the windows bigger than in earlier baths, the sauna (*laconicum*) re-introduced, and a bigger gym and sunbathing facilities provided. Unfortunately, no Pompeian ever had the pleasure of bathing in the Central Baths as they were not finished by the time of the eruption in AD 79. In fact, in the last moments, workmen had just begun putting up the expensive marble columns around the finished shell of the building.

The men's changing room (*apodyterium*) of the Stabian Baths is furnished with stone benches and wall niches for storing the clothes of bathers.

The Suburban Baths

Only recently excavated, the Suburban Baths have revealed a wonderful multi-storey bath complex perfectly integrated into the terraced landscape. Situated just outside the Marine Gate, the rooms of the baths have large picture windows with views of the coast. It has been suggested that the baths extended down the slope to the sea. An inscription mentions thermal baths, which offered seawater bathing to clients, built by Marcus Crassus Frugi, who was consul in AD 64 (he was subsequently killed by Nero). One of the most important features is the splendid painted decoration in the changing room with its erotic frieze of numbered love scenes – the sexual positions it depicts may be a catalogue of services offered by the prostitutes on the top floor.

The views from the large picture windows of the Suburban Baths over the Bay of Naples are as wonderful today as they must have been in AD 79.

The main entrance to the baths was situated on the north side of the porticoed road that led up to the Marine Gate. The entrance opened up into an internal triangular porticoed area. Bathers would change in the *apodyterium* and move through into the cold room. To the east was a large swimming pool with walls painted with scenes of the Nile. The pool was filled from a pretty fountain playing in the adjacent alcove (*nymphaeum*), which cascaded down a small marble staircase to fill the pool. The tepidarium is situated to the north of the cold room and heated by under-floor and wall heating. A doorway to the east gives access to the *laconicum*, which has the usual four apses set into the walls. Next door to this, and to the north, is the hot room (*caldarium*), which also has under-floor and wall heating. The walls were ornamented with numerous apses and niches that may have held marble statues. The views from the large picture windows in the west apse must have been wonderful as they over-looked the Bay of Naples. Next to the *caldarium* there was a heated antechamber that led to a large heated swimming pool, again surrounded by walls decorated with apses and niches, no doubt with numerous marble statues. From the south side of the complex a staircase led to the upper floor, where there were a number of rooms on the west side with service rooms and kitchens behind them.

The baths were probably built in the late first century BC by a local entrepreneur and, although damaged in the earthquake of AD 62, were in the process of being rebuilt. It is thought that both the forum and Stabian Baths were completely rebuilt and refurbished after the earthquake of AD 62. The Stabian Baths still needed repairs to the water supply, but the Forum Baths were certainly operating for male bathers at the time of the eruption. More interestingly, vast sums of money were being spent on a huge new bathing complex in Region IX: the Central Baths show that the town itself, or private benefactors, were still in a position to fund very expensive building projects in a country town.

PRIVATE HOMES

Pompeii and Herculaneum have been so well preserved that they provide the most complete picture we have of the architecture and way of life of the Roman empire, from the fourth century BC until the volcanic eruption in AD 79. Houses in both cities had been badly damaged by the earthquake of AD 62, but many had been rebuilt and embellished by their owners with the most up-to-date decoration.

Opposite **The House of the Vettii is one of the most important private homes in Pompeii. It had been extensively refurbished after the earthquake of AD 62. The nineteenth-century excavator of the building took the controversial decision to leave everything in its place, as found.**

The houses were designed to look inwards, like most housing today in the eastern Mediterranean. There were few windows on the outside, the light to illuminate the interior of the building coming from internal courtyards. These contained fountains and formal gardens embellished with fine statues. The interior of the house was cool and peaceful, protected from the noise and dust of the streets beyond.

GRAND HOUSE ARCHITECTURE

The basic floor plan of a Roman house was described in the modern translation of *The Ten Books of Architecture* by Vitruvius, dating from the first century BC. Although the measurements and proportions of Pompeiian houses often differ from the examples given by Vitruvius, the principles are worth noting: 'Winter dining rooms and bathrooms should have a south-western exposure, for the reason that they need the evening light, and also because the setting sun, facing them in all its splendour but with abated heat, lends a gentler warmth to that quarter in the evening. Bedrooms and libraries ought to have an eastern exposure, because their purposes require the morning light' (Vitruvius, *The Ten Books of Architecture*, VI.I.1–2). Houses often provided a *vestibulum* between the front door and the street. This was a public area where clients could await the call to the morning *salutatio*, where they would offer their petitions or congratulations to their patron. The passage leading from the front entrance, the *fauces* or 'throat' of the house, led into the main reception room (*atrium*). Vitruvius notes that the *atrium* is a public area, 'which any of the people have a perfect right to enter, even without an invitation'. The *atrium* was necessary only if the household was important, for 'men of everyday fortune do not need entrance courts, or atriums built in grand style, because such men are more apt to discharge their social obligations by going round to others than to have others come to them' (Vitruvius, op. cit., V.2).

The *atrium* courtyard was sometimes entirely covered, as at the House of the Stags at Herculaneum and the House of the Ephebe at Pompeii. It was equipped with a central skylight, gutters and drainpipes that directed the rainwater from the roof to the basin below (*compluvium/impluvium*).

Vitruvius wrote that the *atrium* had originally been the principal room of the house and an appropriate area to locate the shrine to the household

The House of Menander, showing its classical layout of vestibule, *atrium* and *tablinum*, and beyond to the peristyle garden and *exedra*.

gods (*lararium*). Occasionally the *atrium* was adorned with the smoke-blackened portrait busts of the owners' ancestors, suggesting it was an enclosed space and the soot from lamps had blackened the portrait busts. However, the origins of the *atrium* may have been as an open courtyard in front of the house, as found in Mediterranean houses from as early as 2000 BC. Either side of the *atrium* and at the end furthest from the entrance were rooms called *alae* that may have originally contained the portrait busts of the ancestors, but were more usually waiting rooms for clients or offices for secretaries. These sometimes had an exterior window to let in extra light to the *atrium* or, sometimes, access to an exterior doorway.

The *tablinum*, usually located on the main axis of the building, was a large room opening on to the rear of the *atrium*. The *tablinum* was, architecturally, the most impressive room in the *atrium* complex and was considered the central room of the house. Originally the master bedroom, it was also used as a reception room, study, office and dining room. Wooden screens, folding doors or curtains ensured privacy when the patron (*patronus*) required it. This was where his clients, parasites and camp followers 'saluted' (*salutatio*) the patron, and asked for either presents and handouts or support for their plans, dreams and aspirations.

A number of *cubicula*, or sleeping chambers, opened off the *atrium*. These could be used for private interviews between patron and client, or as guest bedrooms. Pliny the Younger notes that his uncle, Pliny the Elder, slept in a *cubiculum* in the house of Pomponius at Stabiae on the night of the eruption of Vesuvius.

The dining room (*triclinium*), or dining rooms, could be situated in various areas of the house depending on the season. In the summer meals could be eaten in the garden room, and at other times the rooms either side of the *tablinum* could be used. Meals were an important event for the Roman household. The word *triclinium* literally means 'three couches'. Each couch held three people and the placing of guests was important, as indeed it is today. The dining rooms were small and it was certainly a squeeze to fit in three couches, let alone the attendant slaves. Slaves would receive the arriving guests, and their duties and the behaviour expected of guests was inscribed on the wall of the winter dining room by the owner of the House of the Moralist: 'The slave shall wash and dry the feet of the guest; and let him be sure to spread a linen cloth on the cushions of the couches. Don't cast lustful glances or make eyes at another man's wife. Don't be coarse in your conversation. Restrain yourself from getting angry or using offensive language. If you cannot, go back to your own house!'

Diners reclined on richly embroidered cushions whilst enjoying meals comprising many courses. A full dinner started with antipasto (*gustatio*) with eggs, sea food, vegetables, and honeyed wine, followed by *prima cena*, the fish, meat and vegetable course in which a number of separate dishes would be served. Then came *secunda cena,* with dessert, sweetmeats and both fresh and dried fruit. Wine was usually diluted with water and then

The unusual summer dining room of the *praedia* of Julia Felix. Within the *nymphaeum* setting, the diners would recline on cushioned benches surrounded by waterfalls and cascades.

flavoured and in the winter it was normally warmed. Excavators found a wine heater in the House of the Fruit Orchard. The only cutlery available was spoons for eating shellfish and eggs. Instead diners would help themselves to food already cut up by the servants. The food would be taken from the dish with the left hand and eaten with the right hand. Slaves would offer finger bowls and towels to wash sticky fingers, except in more affluent homes where the dining room had little channels of running water in front of the couches. The three couches were usually arranged in a U-shape with a low table in the centre. Men and women ate together, although earlier in the Roman period women sat at the table while the men reclined. For extra comfort, some couches sloped upward at one end. Dinner started around 4 pm and could last well into the evening. It was usually a leisurely social occasion with entertainment provided by musicians, poets, dancers and tumbling dwarfs.

Houses at Pompeii and Herculaneum were extended by building a second *atrium*, which allowed more room for the domestic activities of the household. The second *atrium* was normally smaller than the first, and the inward-sloping roof was supported by columns (the *tetrastyle* arrangement), whereas its predecessor lacked columns and was more open (tuscanic). The second *atrium* did not have a *tablinum* and the rooms opening on to it were the *cubicula* and *alae,* most often used as reception rooms or additional bedrooms. The final development of the town house was the addition of an internal courtyard flanked on its sides by a colonnade or a row of piers that looked out over an ornamental garden (peristyle). The peristyle became so fashionable that owners of houses with insufficient space for a complete peristyle would build a pseudo-peristyle of one or two porticos (a roof supported by columns). The remaining solid walls would be decorated with a stucco or painted colonnade with a mural of a garden scene in the intervening spaces to give the illusion of a garden beyond.

ROMAN GARDENS

The *atrium* and peristyle were arranged along the central axis of the house and sometimes the architect would alter the distances between columns to create false perspectives, making the peristyle appear larger than it actually was. The peristyle was the most private part of the house and, whilst the Greeks had decorated their peristyle courtyards with mosaics, in Pompeii and Herculaneum the garden was an essential feature. A careful mix of water and plants was extremely important to the Roman householder. Greek horticulturalists (*topiarii*) had been at work in Italy from the second century BC creating magnificent gardens on the estates of Scipio Africanus and Decimus Junius Brutus. Formal beds were enclosed by beaten-earth paths where medicinal plants and vegetables were grown. Vines on trellises intermingled with ponds; fountains and running water were enhanced with statues, sundials and masks while decorative discs tinkled in the wind. The garden was a sanctuary and a place for contemplation. In some gardens a shrine (*lararium*) was found dedicated to the god Bacchus, who was the god of vegetation as well as of wine. Bacchus promised his followers paradise after death, and the symbol of earthly paradise was the garden.

The wonderful formal garden of Loreius Tiburtinus (II.2.2) constructed around a whole series of ornamental pools, with pergolas and shrines surrounded by fruit trees and acanthus plants.

The garden room (*exedra*) usually adjoined the peristyle garden. A large room used for entertaining and dining, it was often decorated with paintings of animals, birds and plants, continuing and extending the '*hortus*' theme from the adjoining garden.

With the building of the peristyle, there was even less room for service areas and slave quarters, and some of these areas were relegated to the upper floors of the house. The kitchen (*culina*), found at the back of the house, was small and within this cramped area was a raised hearth with a wood or charcoal fire surmounted by metal trivets where cooking pots and pans could be placed. Some kitchens would also have a small oven for baking bread. There may have been a sink too, which might have had piped water from the town aqueduct. Behind a partition wall, but in the same room, there was usually a private toilet; which would have been flushed using rainwater and would have emptied into a cesspit. They were also useful for disposing of kitchen waste.

The peristyle garden of the House of the Faun. The garden was formally arranged, with an elegant fountain and basin set within borders of box hedges.

HOUSE DECORATION

Goethe, the nineteenth-century German traveller and writer, said that the deaths of the cities of Pompeii and Herculaneum were significant not for the brevity of life but for the perpetuity of art. Art played an important part in the lives of the inhabitants of Pompeii; although they lived in a provincial area, they were surrounded by decoration that had meaning. The architecture complemented the frescoes, mosaics, stucco reliefs and sculptures in such a way that it gives us an understanding of how the Romans lived. We can see the cruelty of the gladiatorial contests, observe human desires and fantasies at the brothels and try to understand the secret rites of initiation into the cult of Dionysus at the Villa of the Mysteries. The most exciting experience, however, is seeing this art in the rooms or buildings just as the people of Pompeii and Herculaneum would have viewed it.

The exquisite fourth-style paintings in the dining room just off the peristyle garden of the House of the Vettii show a wonderful selection of mythological scenes.

To help understand the chronological development of Pompeiian wall painting, the scholar August Mau, writing in 1882, established that there were four styles. The definition of these four styles is still in use today. The name of one painter has survived from the many that must have painted at Pompeii. Pliny the Younger wrote that a painter called Studius, who lived at the time of Augustus, introduced to Pompeii 'the delightful style of decorating walls with representations of villas, harbours, landscape gardens, sacred groves, woods, hills, fish ponds, straits, streams and shores, any scene in short that took his fancy' (*Natural History*, IX.33–35).

To create these wonderful paintings the wall had to be prepared with up to three coats of fine plaster. The background of the picture was painted first and left to dry. The figures and decoration were then added, the paint mixture probably including glue and wax to give a shine to the surface, which was also polished. The subject matter was seldom original, but there were no copyright laws in ancient Rome and most paintings (and some sculptures) were derived from Greek originals. The more famous the original Greek artist, the more he seems to have been copied.

The first style (according to August Mau) of painting dates from the late third century to the early first century BC. It imitates variegated marble, porphyry or alabaster relief marble walls. Occasionally called the 'incrustation style', it was executed in stucco relief and then painted and polished to resemble colourful marble walling. The best examples can be

An imaginary garden (*paradeisos*) painted in the third style on to the *oecus* of the House of the Wedding of Alexander in Pompeii (VI.17.42). The marble basin is surrounded by birds and framed by two garden statues called *herms*.

found in the basilica, the House of the Faun, and the Temple of Jupiter at Pompeii. Painting in this style sometimes displayed small architectural features that became more widespread and evolved into the second style of painting. Also known as the 'architectural style', it overlapped with the first style and dated from the end of the second century to the beginning of the first century BC. The wall paintings were much more theatrical with the image frequently divided into three areas – top, middle and bottom. The middle area was divided vertically with columns. Vitruvius wrote that theatrical *scaena* influenced Roman interiors: 'Tragic scenes are delineated with columns, pediments, statues' (*De Architecture*, V.8).

The use of such architectural motifs made the wall seem three-dimensional. Windows were painted on to the walls and seemed to open on to vistas which were made to appear distant by the use of misty contours and diminishing colours. The best example of this is probably shown by the wonderful series of paintings found in the atrium at the Villa of Mysteries, just outside Pompeii. The pictures are divided from one another by thin columns, which give the room the appearance of a pergola looking

A formal Roman garden painted on an internal wall of a house at Pompeii. The painting endeavours to extend the illusion of an imaginary garden in a restricted space.

out onto the vistas of other columned halls, streets and houses. The paintings introduce another element of the second style, which is the vista of a rural arcadia shown through an illusionary opening painted into the architectural framework. The subject matter for these paintings ranged from flocks and herds shepherded by rustics in a timeless landscape, to formal parks with pavilions and shrines. Clients sometimes wished their own garden to be painted, either as it was or, more usually, how it should be. Painting pictures of flowers, extended gardens, shrubs and birds on the surrounding walls gave the illusion of extending the garden and therefore making it look larger. The idea was not a new one; Greek painters had been warming to the theme from at least the second century BC. Demetrius, the son of Seleucus – the first landscape painter whose name is known – had been painting in Rome from 164 BC, and was called a *topographos* (landscape painter). Some of the best examples are in the *atrium* of the House of Fabius Amandio (I.7.2–3), where a group of three birds sits on the rim of a marble birdbath, and also a little further afield at the Villa of Poppaea at Oplontis.

Another new pictorial element introduced in the second style is the representation of monumental figures within architectural frameworks called megalography by historians. The best example is the stunning series of paintings found in the *triclinium* (dining room) of the Villa of Mysteries, just outside the Herculaneum Gate at Pompeii. The villa, a huge 90-room mansion, contains the most famous of all Pompeiian paintings. The decoration consists of 29 life-size figures seemingly involved in rites associated with Bacchus. They show the preparations for a wedding, the scourging of a woman, the playing of a lyre, women dancing and so on. The figures seem totally preoccupied and almost in a spiritual trance, completely oblivious to the outside world. It has been said that the people in the paintings seem entirely absorbed in their own existence, engrossed in their pursuits and abiding in a world apart from ours. It seems that the bride-to-be has to undergo terrible torments of a physical and sexual nature to win salvation with the cult of Bacchus. The date of the painting

Part of the cycle of Dionysian rites second-style paintings from the Villa of Mysteries. On the left, Silenus gives a drink to a pair of young satyrs.

has yet to be confirmed; it could be from the time of Caesar or from the early part of the reign of Augustus.

It is likely that the third style of painting, also known as 'ornamental', developed under Augustus and continued until the reign of Claudius (20 BC to AD 40–60). The style is simpler and more organised than the second style. The walls are more solid, with far fewer dramatic architectural motifs. The central panel was usually painted quite dark, occasionally black, and the painting in the centre of the panel had become much smaller and was usually 'mounted' on ornate and intricate painted candelabras. The borders of the panels were delicate frames of foliage arabesques, candelabras, masks and ribbons. One of the best examples is in the *tablinum* of the House of Marcus Lucretius Fronto (IV.V.4–10) where the top part of the wall was painted in a delicate architectural fantasy, similar to the backdrop (*scaenae frons*) of a theatre. Below the central panels the dado painting showed a marvellous garden, complete with garden walls in white marble and embellished with an urn fountain and white marble benches.

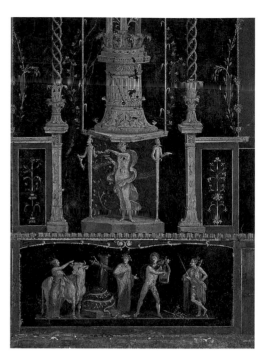

A detail of the wall decoration in the dining room of the House of the Vettii, painted in the fourth style. The lower panel (shown enlarged overleaf) portrays scenes from the tragic play *Iphigenia among the Taurians* by Euripides.

The fourth style of painting covers a whole host of different styles and types and is occasionally called the 'fantastic' or 'illusionist' style. There are numerous examples in Pompeii and Herculaneum because the fourth style of painting was being used at the time of the earthquake of AD 62. The extensive restoration and repainting that followed the serious damage it caused meant much work was done in the fourth style. It has been estimated that up to 17 painters were at work in Pompeii following the earthquake.

The fourth style is a pot-pourri of elements from the second and third styles with the incorporation of stucco reliefs into the paintings, as seen in the Stabian and Forum Baths at Pompeii. The architectural structures in the paintings appear unreal and the decoration fussy. Some of the better examples of this style of painting can be found in the House of the Tragic Poet (VI.8.5), the House of Loreius Tiburtinus (II.8.5) and the House of the Vettii (VI.15.1), which has a wonderful painting on the east wall of the *triclinium* (dining room), depicting the punishment of Ixion, a story of infidelity, betrayal and punishment.

A scene from *Iphigenia among the Taurians* by Euripides, part of a decorative panel in the House of the Vettii (see previous page).

The dates given for the four styles of painting can only be approximate. Clients' tastes must have changed slowly and painters were probably reluctant to discard a style of painting at which they were adept. There has been much discussion about whether the wall paintings of Pompeii are true 'frescoes' – that is, painted rapidly on to recently applied damp plaster. A large room, recently excavated at the House of the Chaste Lovers (I.10.11) was in the process of being painted at the time of the eruption. The technique being used, in this case, was unquestionably fresco, but it is difficult to tell in other cases.

It was obviously the aim of the architect to cover the floors of Pompeian houses with decoration that complemented the wall paintings and emphasised the status of the owner. The medium used for floor decoration was the mosaic, which has become synonymous with Roman floors throughout the empire. The earliest mosaics at Pompeii and Herculaneum are to be found in the *atria* of the large Samnite houses, such as the House of the Faun (VI.12.2-5) in Pompeii and the House of the Mosaic Atrium at Herculaneum. These mosaics are usually a simple geometric pattern of black and white marble cubes (*tesserae*).

Some remarkable examples of the older Greek carpet technique have been found, where the mosaic is in the form of a picture rather than an overall decorative pattern. One of the best examples is the famous mosaic floor, found in 1831 at the House of the Faun, depicting Alexander the Great in battle. The year after the discovery of the mosaic Goethe wrote:

'The present and the future will not succeed in commenting correctly on this artistic marvel, and we must always return, after having studied and explained it, to simple, pure wonder.' The battle portrayed might not be Issus in 333 BC, but the rout of the Persians at Gaugamela in 331. It is usually thought that the mosaic is based on a Greek painting for King Cassander (305–297 BC), possibly by Philoxenus of Eretria. Recently, however, it has been suggested that it may have been commissioned by Selencos (who is portrayed as a footsoldier at Alexander's side) for a building at Antioch.

The House of the Faun is one of the most magnificent residences in Pompeii. Covering a whole block (its ground area is some 3,000 square metres/32,290 square feet), it is also the largest house in Pompeii. The mosaic was found in the *exedra*, a room with a view out into the peristyle

The view from the *atrium* at the House of the Faun through the *tablinum* to the peristyle and garden beyond. The statue of the satyr, found originally beside the pool, gives the house its erroneous name.

A silver goblet found at Boscoreale, decorated with skeletons beneath garlands of roses. One of the skeletons is seen weighing a purse against a butterfly, symbolic of the human soul. The purse is labelled 'Wisdom'.

garden used for entertaining guests. The walls of the *exedra* were decorated in the architectural first style, with a stucco frieze portraying the centaurs at Pirithous' wedding feast that can be dated to the fourth century BC. Two Corinthian columns flanked the doorway and the floor was decorated in mosaic with scenes from the Nile. The mosaic floor of the *exedra* was executed in two types of mosaic. The border to the pictorial mosaic was laid in white marble cubes of about 1 centimetre ($^1/_2$ inch) square, and the same large tesserae were used in the frame surrounding the pictorial mosaic. The battle scene and the four floral corner motifs were executed with extremely small tesserae – on average, each one is 3 millimetres ($^1/_8$ inch) square – and there are over 4 million individual cubes in the mosaic. The colouring of them is that which is naturally found in the type of limestone used. Close examination of the mosaic has revealed that at some time in antiquity it had been cut into two parts and transported to Pompeii, possibly from an area recently conquered by the Romans. It is all too apparent that the *exedra* in which it was located is far too small to contain it. Guests standing at the doorway, on the mosaic decorated with a Nile landscape, would not have been able to see the whole battle scene, and if they stepped back to get a better view they would have found the Corinthian columns in the way. The damage to the left half of the mosaic may have been caused by the eruption of AD 79, or possibly by the lifting of the mosaic in the nineteenth century to transport it to the Archaeological Museum in Naples.

LIFE AND DEATH

Wall paintings and mosaics completely covered and decorated the interiors of Pompeiian houses. Furniture was sparse and would have distracted attention from the grand internal designs, but the furniture that was used – couches, tables, lamp stands, folding chairs – was magnificent. The use of bronze mountings chased with gold and silver inlay, precious woods, ivory, tortoiseshell and coral show that the craftsmen who made such objects were imbued with skill and ability. Goethe, when visiting Pompeii, was enthralled with the 'high, slender bronze pedestals, evidently intended as lamp stands, with feet shaped into claws or hooves and sometimes adjustable sliding upper parts'.

Silverware was also very fine, and has been found in many of the grand houses. In 1895, at a country villa called La Pisanella in Boscoreale, 108 embossed silver vessels were discovered and, in 1930, a small boy exploring at the House of Menander at Pompeii (I.10.4) found 118 silver vessels and objects all carefully wrapped in canvas hidden in a half-buried chest. Recent research indicates the collection came from far and wide. Pliny remarked that silver was the preferred medium for famous artists to show their ability. Certainly the silverware found at Pompeii shows extraordinary skill, with the subject matter ranging from cups decorated with skeletons to quite intricate pastoral scenes.

Death was given due respect in Pompeiian society. This mosaic shows a skull, with the soul of the departed, represented by a butterfly, sitting on the wheel of fortune below. Balanced by the scale above the skull are symbols of wealth and poverty: on the left a rich man's purple toga and a sceptre, on the right a beggar's rags, knapsack and crook.

To entertain well, it was important to have impressive silverware, glasses for drinking, bone-handled knives, high-quality pottery, good food and live entertainment. The people of Pompeii and Herculaneum had developed a rich and diverse world of work and play. The doomed population of both cities lived life to the full; a contemporary poet wrote:

Now the crickets pierce the thickets with their repetitive cry, now even the speckled lizard takes shelter in the coolness of the garden. If you are wise, lie back and make a libation with summer weight glassware, or if you wish, we will bring out the new goblets of crystal. Come, you are weary, rest in the grape arbour and bind your heavy head with a chaplet of roses. Cull kisses from a tender maidservant. Forget about those who raise old-fashioned eyebrows! Why keep fragrant garlands for ungrateful ashes? Do you want your bones to lie under a garland-carved stone? Set out the wine and the dice. To hell with him who cares for the morrow. Death plucks your ear and says, 'Live now, for I am on my way!'
(*Appendix Vergiliana Copa*, 35–51)

And death was on its way. In the Via dell'Abbondanza, Pompeii's main shopping street, stands one of the biggest houses. It covers an area of 992 square metres (10,600 square feet). Now called the House of Julius Polybius (IX.13.3), it is named after the numerous election graffiti on its façade promoting the virtues of the *duumvir* of the same name. The house was built on two levels, with 37 rooms on the ground floor and 19 on the first floor, and is a combination of at least two older houses. An *atrium* was built where there used to be the peristyle garden (*viridarium*), giving an unusual sequence of rooms. The main entrance was on the east side of the austere frontage adjacent to a shop. The vestibule led to a covered courtyard ornamented with wonderful first style architectural decorations, including a painted imitation door. The original *tablinum* to the north of the covered courtyard was converted into an antechamber. The *atrium* was paved with a cobbled floor and the *impluvium* had a base of coloured marble pieces enhanced with a diamond pattern of white marble tesserae. On the west side of the *atrium* was a series of *cubicula* separated from the kitchen by a corridor leading to it and a staircase to the upper floors. On the north side of the *atrium* was the *tablinum* with views through to the peristyle with its three porticoed sides and garden planted with fruit trees.

Beyond this was a further set of rooms, including a *triclinium* and another *cubiculum*. The decoration of these rooms was in the third style. Of particular interest are the ceiling decorations – some of the rare examples to have survived. Numerous items of household furniture were found stored here while the house was undergoing restoration. These included a set of clothes chests found under the east portico and the bronze statue of a youth that was used as a lamp holder. In the *triclinium*, the remains of the bronze dining couches and banqueting service were found scattered on the floor. A bronze signet ring inscribed 'C. IULI PHILIPPI' was found in one of the clothes chests put out in the peristyle (probably to make room for the restoration work that was going on indoors), suggesting that a relative called Caius Julius Philippus might have stayed with the family recently.

The excavators also found 13 human skeletons, all of them gathered in two rooms on the ground floor at the back of the house. In the first room, six adults and one foetus were found in the ash. One of the adults was a woman clasping a valuable bronze vase and a cloth bag full of silver and

Although only about 20 bronze lamps have been found at Pompeii, the variety and excellence of their craftsmanship is staggering. This dancing figure holding aloft the lampholder is a typical example of how beautiful these objects can be.

bronze coins. She was wearing a pair of gold earrings and two gold bracelets, one on either arm. She was also wearing two gold rings, one with a brown and one with a violet stone. She was aged between 45 and 50 years old, 158 centimetres (5 feet 2 inches) tall, her teeth were worn, some were lost, and her bones showed signs of arthritis. It is likely she was the wife of Polybius. Next to her lay her daughter, aged between 16 and 18 years. Her graceful bones were heavily stained green, indicating contact with lots of jewels. She was 145 centimetres (4 feet 9 inches) tall and she suffered from spina bifida, a genetic malformation. She was also heavily pregnant, the skeleton of her baby was found in her abdomen. The baby was in its ninth or tenth month since conception. Another skeleton, a male, lay nearby with his mouth open, slumped with his head leaning close to the wall. His right arm was bent with his

The bewitching hour – nighttime in a Pompeiian garden lit only by candles and oil lamps.

hand on his chest and his left arm outstretched apparently for a little glass bottle. It is possible that the glass bottle held poison. The rest of the family group lay nearby, or in the other room. A pet turtle lay dead in the garden outside.

On the day of the volcanic eruption, 24 August AD 79, the household waited for the pumice to stop raining down. It never stopped and as the roofs started to collapse they retired to the strongest rooms at the back of the house. By the morning, nearly 3 metres (10 feet) of pumice had accumulated outside in the garden and it was too late to escape. At around 7.30 am on 25 August the fourth surge of hot volcanic material hit Pompeii killing everything in its path. Julius Polybius, his wife, his daughter, his son-in-law, his unborn grandchild and the rest of his family, and thousands of unnamed people in Pompeii and Herculaneum, having suffered dreadfully, were now dead.

A DAY'S GUIDE TO POMPEII

The ancient city of Pompeii is spread across a huge area with all kinds of public buildings, temples, shops and bars that once served its population. Even though only part of the city has been excavated, Pompeii is still one of the largest archaeological sites in the world with a great variety of structures to see and understand. For this reason, we have selected some of the city's highlights and arranged them into an itinerary that should be sufficient to occupy you for a full day – depending on how long you choose to spend at each place.

Opposite **The peristyle and garden of the House of Venus in the Sea Shell. On the far wall is the famous painting of Venus from which the house takes its name.**

Throughout this guide, we have used the identification system devised by Giuseppe Fiorelli to catalogue the areas of the city and the individual buildings and structures within them. Director of excavations from 1860 to 1875, he introduced order to the archaeological work by dividing the town into nine areas called regions. Each region was sub-divided into 'blocks' called *insulae* and the structures within the *insulae* were individually numbered as houses. A Roman numeral identifies each region; the *insulae* and houses are numbered in Arabic numerals. For example, the House of the Vettii is in region VI, *insula* 15, and the house number is 1; so its identification is VI.15.1. Wherever possible, the identification number is usually to be found on a plaque attached to the front of each building. Please note that buildings may be closed to the public at certain times of the year or day.

Do check the facilities when you enter the site; at the time of writing the only café is near the Forum Baths and this is also the location of the only toilets on site, apart from those at the Marine Gate entrance. A day walking around will be tiring, so remember to dress suitably and take water.

START FROM THE MARINE GATE
The main entrance to the site is at the Marine Gate. Here you can purchase your entrance ticket and find useful information and a shop. On the left before entering the Roman gateway are the remains of the Suburban Baths (page 138).

To the right is the so-called Imperial Villa, built against the city walls. The villa's portico is supported by 41 brick columns faced with fluted white stucco. The back wall was decorated with small paintings and elegant figured medallions, which were unfortunately removed by the eighteenth-century excavators. The road to the Marine Gate is steep and was unsuitable for Roman wheeled traffic. There are two entrances through the gate: the one on the left was for pedestrians, the larger one, on the right, for pack animals. Double doors could close off both entrances.

TEMPLE OF VENUS
Continue to the top of the hill and turn to your right. You will enter a wide flat area with extensive views over the countryside and sea to the south. The loveliest temple in Pompeii once stood here. It was dedicated to Venus Pompeiana, the patroness of the city. Built in 80 BC after Roman colonists had been settled in Pompeii by the Roman general Sulla, the temple, constructed in white marble, was one of the finest monuments in the city and visible from afar. It is now almost completely destroyed, with only fragments of architectural decoration remaining.

TEMPLE OF APOLLO
Retrace your steps to the top of the hill and further ahead on your left is the Temple of Apollo (page 115), situated in an area enclosed by a portico of 48 columns. The *cella*, or shrine, sits on a high podium surrounded by a Corinthian colonnade with six columns to the front. The earliest material on the site dates from 575–550 BC. Two bronze statues flank the façade of the temple, Apollo to the right and a bust of Diana to the left; both deities are portrayed as archers. The temple's altar is situated in front of the staircase leading up to the temple and on the left is a column with a sundial, which was added in the time of Augustus.

THE FORUM
To the right of the Temple of Apollo is the forum (page 111). The structure we see today dates from the second half of the second century BC. This great rectangular square measures 142 metres (466 feet) by 37 metres (124 feet). It is lined with the most important religious, commercial and political buildings in the city and was closed to Roman traffic. Its final architectural form was established during the time of Augustus and it is dominated by the Temple of Jupiter at the far north end. Opposite, ranging along the south side of the forum, are the three municipal offices (page 113). Walk to the centre of the square and face the remains of the Temple of Jupiter, the most imposing building facing the forum.

TEMPLE OF JUPITER
Immediately in front of you is the Temple of Jupiter (page 113). It dates from the second century BC, but was rebuilt, in the years following the arrival of the Roman colonists in 80 BC, into a *Capitolium* and dedicated to Jupiter, Juno and Minerva, the deities of the Capitoline triad. It was a building of breathtaking beauty that dominated the square, with vistas

opening up through the triumphal arch on the right to the grand houses to the north of the square.

MACELLUM

Parallel to the Temple of Jupiter, in the north-east corner of the forum, is the *macellum* (page 123). The building was used as a public market selling fish and meat. Attached to it are over 30 shops, all with their counters facing north so their produce was in the shade and did not deteriorate in the hot sun. In the centre of the market are 12 pillars of stone, which supported the wooden poles of a pavilion. The pavilion was used to clean the fish sold in the area to the right of the shrine situated on the rear wall, which contained a statue of the emperor. On the left of the shrine there was a room that may have been used for banquets

The view of Vesuvius is framed by the remains of the imperial triumphal arch adjacent to the Temple of Jupiter.

to honour the imperial cult. Under cover on the north-east wall, some wall paintings in the fourth style (page 153) have survived. The panels contain scenes from mythology, in this case Medea mourning the death of her

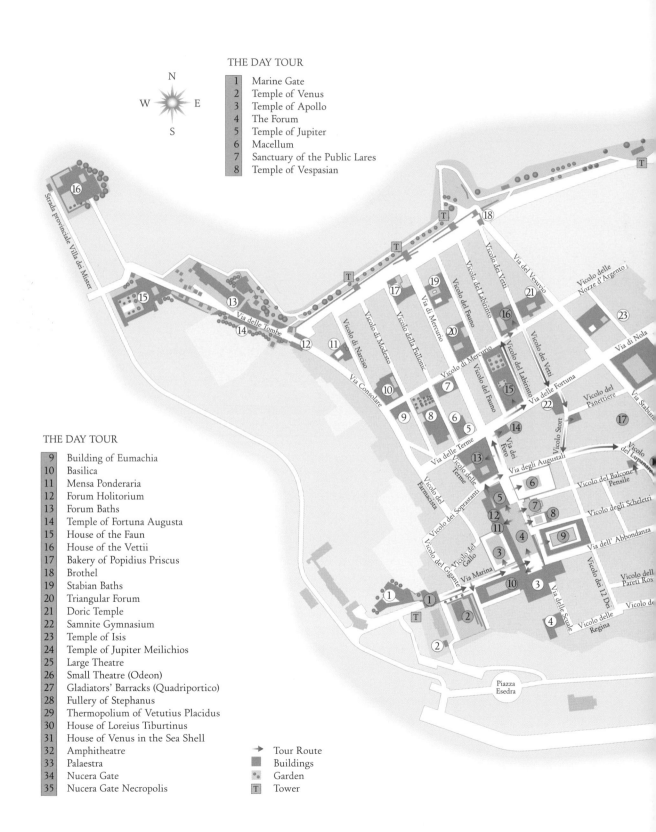

N
W — E
S

THE DAY TOUR

1	Marine Gate
2	Temple of Venus
3	Temple of Apollo
4	The Forum
5	Temple of Jupiter
6	Macellum
7	Sanctuary of the Public Lares
8	Temple of Vespasian

THE DAY TOUR

9	Building of Eumachia
10	Basilica
11	Mensa Ponderaria
12	Forum Holitorium
13	Forum Baths
14	Temple of Fortuna Augusta
15	House of the Faun
16	House of the Vettii
17	Bakery of Popidius Priscus
18	Brothel
19	Stabian Baths
20	Triangular Forum
21	Doric Temple
22	Samnite Gymnasium
23	Temple of Isis
24	Temple of Jupiter Meilichios
25	Large Theatre
26	Small Theatre (Odeon)
27	Gladiators' Barracks (Quadriportico)
28	Fullery of Stephanus
29	Thermopolium of Vetutius Placidus
30	House of Loreius Tiburtinus
31	House of Venus in the Sea Shell
32	Amphitheatre
33	Palaestra
34	Nucera Gate
35	Nucera Gate Necropolis

→ Tour Route
■ Buildings
⋮ Garden
T Tower

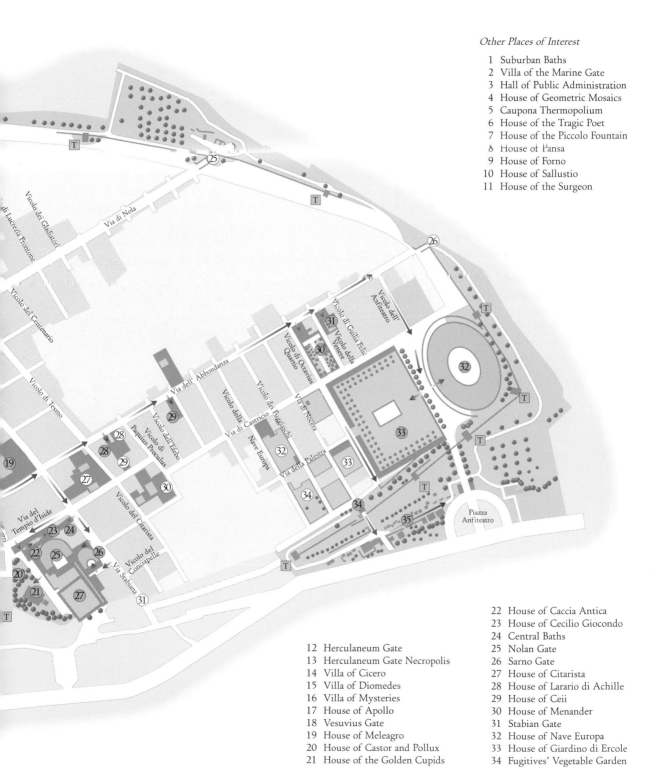

Other Places of Interest

1 Suburban Baths
2 Villa of the Marine Gate
3 Hall of Public Administration
4 House of Geometric Mosaics
5 Caupona Thermopolium
6 House of the Tragic Poet
7 House of the Piccolo Fountain
8 House of Pansa
9 House of Forno
10 House of Sallustio
11 House of the Surgeon

12 Herculaneum Gate
13 Herculaneum Gate Necropolis
14 Villa of Cicero
15 Villa of Diomedes
16 Villa of Mysteries
17 House of Apollo
18 Vesuvius Gate
19 House of Meleagro
20 House of Castor and Pollux
21 House of the Golden Cupids

22 House of Caccia Antica
23 House of Cecilio Giocondo
24 Central Baths
25 Nolan Gate
26 Sarno Gate
27 House of Citarista
28 House of Larario di Achille
29 House of Ceii
30 House of Menander
31 Stabian Gate
32 House of Nave Europa
33 House of Giardino di Ercole
34 Fugitives' Vegetable Garden

children, Io and Argos, and another one portraying Penelope recognising Ulysses.

SANCTUARY OF THE PUBLIC LARES

Next door to the *macellum* is the Temple or Sanctuary of the Public Lares (page 121), one of the most unusual public buildings in Pompeii. Numerous theories have been postulated regarding not only its function, but also when it was built. The building has an open area, almost square, once decorated with a magnificent floor of cut marble slabs patterned in alternating framed squares and circles.

There was an altar erected in the centre of the floor with part of the plinth still remaining. Numerous niches around the walls undoubtedly once held important statues of the imperial family. Most of the magnificent decoration has now gone, probably stolen by robbers after the volcanic eruption in AD 79.

TEMPLE OF VESPASIAN

The next building to the south on the same road is the Temple of Vespasian (page 117), which celebrates the Imperial cult. The exterior of the building is faced with marble panels

that date from the restoration work carried out in Pompeii after the devastating earthquake of AD 62. As you enter the building there is a narrow portico leading into an open courtyard with a magnificent, white marble sacrificial altar in the centre. The shrine proper is in the form of a miniature temple set against the back wall, with steps leading up from both sides. The four columns at the

The entrance to the building of Eumachia, framed by a marble frieze carved with acanthus voT utes with insects, birds and snakes.

front held up the roof under which resided a statue of the emperor. The altar was decorated with a sacrificial scene on the side facing the forum and dates, stylistically, from the time of Augustus.

BUILDING OF EUMACHIA

Continuing south along the road, the next structure is the Building of Eumachia (page 119). Built towards the end of the first century BC, it has been suggested it was either the headquarters of the fullers' guild or used as a slave market, or possibly both. The magnificently decorated central entrance is embellished with a marble portal decorated with acanthus volutes in relief and ornamented with insects, birds and snakes. As you enter the building, you will see to your right a small room with a large terracotta pot built into a platform. It was reputedly used to collect urine used by the fullers as bleach. Ahead of you is a large open courtyard surrounded by a portico with Corinthian columns. On the far side there is a large apse. Now only the brick structure remains, but originally it was faced in marble. The apse once held a statue representing the Empress Livia, the wife of Augustus, as an example of imperial harmony and devotion holding a *cornucopia* (horn of plenty) in her arms. On either side of the large apse there were two small gardens that could be seen from the windows of the apse, possibly planted to continue the theme of abundance of the statue of Livia. Behind the portico there runs a covered gallery and in the area

behind the large apse stands a marble statue of the priestess Eumachia, who built the complex and dedicated it to the *concordia Augusta*, referring to the 'harmony' and 'agreement' within the imperial family. That the statue of Eumachia stands in an intentionally secluded area, just behind the statue of Livia, does suggest that Eumachia hoped her civic activities might be rewarded.

BASILICA

Cross the square to the west side of the forum and in the far south-west corner is the entrance to the basilica (page 126). The building is the most important in Pompeii. Dating from the second half of the second century BC. It housed the law courts and was the place where business was conducted and contracts issued. Its large hall, with a central nave and two aisles, contained a two-storey, four-sided colonnade with 28 fluted Ionic columns built of shaped bricks and then covered in stucco. The basilica had a huge pitched roof, covered in tiles stamped with the name of a local tile manufacturer and former magistrate – Numerius Popidius.

On the far wall is the tribunal where the magistrates sat. They used a set of wooden stairs to reach the platform. The stairs were removable to protect the magistrates from the wrath of an angry crowd – occasionally their decisions led to riots. The basement room underneath the tribunal probably stored records whilst the two rooms on either side may have been offices.

MENSA PONDERARIA AND FORUM HOLITORIUM

Retrace your steps back into the forum and, keeping to the left, walk along the west portico until you reach a large glass display case built into the wall. This is the *mensa ponderaria* (page 113) where weights and measures were checked. There is a stone bench with nine circular cavities of different capacities for measuring set amounts of goods. Each cavity has a small hole at the bottom that held a plug. Once the goods were measured the contents could be released.

Next to the *mensa* is the *forum holitorium* (page 125) or grain market. It is now used as an archaeological store and it is worth viewing (albeit through the bars) the large amount of material kept here. Further on, through a small door on the left, are the public latrines (page 126). Turn right and walk behind the Temple of Jupiter to the first turning on the left. Turn into the Via dei Foro. On your left are the gift shop, cafeteria, toilets and a shady restaurant.

FORUM BATHS

The entrance to the Forum Baths (page 131) is next to the gift shop. The baths occupy the central part of *insula* VI (VI.5.24) and are surrounded by shops and cafés (*thermopolia*). Built with public funds soon after the arrival of the Roman colonists in 80 BC, the baths were probably the only ones in Pompeii operating at the time of the volcanic eruption in AD 79. The others were probably still undergoing repair following earthquake damage. There were two separate bathing areas for men and women, situated on either side of the furnaces, which supplied hot air and water to both bath suites. The usual sequence of rooms is open to the public: first the changing room, then a circular room containing a cold plunge-bath, followed by the warm room and bath, and finally the hot bath. Outside is an exercise yard surrounded by a colonnade now used as a public restaurant.

TEMPLE OF FORTUNA AUGUSTA

On leaving the Forum Baths turn left, and on the right-hand-side corner are the remains of a wonderful temple built of white marble in the Corinthian style by Marcus Tullius in honour of the Emperor Augustus (page 122). The statue of Fortuna Augusta stood on a raised dais located inside at the far end of the shrine. Stand back and look down the street on your right past the gift shop to the triumphal arch, once covered in white marble slabs and probably dedicated to Augustus. Look to your left and you can see another triumphal arch located on the Via di Mercurio and probably dedicated to Caligula. Both arches would have had statues in all the niches and recesses and were probably topped with a bronze equestrian statue. Turn right into the Via della Fortuna and on your left is the House of the Faun

HOUSE OF THE FAUN (VI.12.2)

Named after the bronze figure of the 'Dancing Faun' (which is in fact a satyr) found on the side of the *impluvium* in the main *atrium* (page 154), this is the largest house in Pompeii and occupies an entire insula. Originally built during

the Samnite period (second century BC), it shows elements of Hellenistic influence in its layout of two *atria*, a peristyle and a spacious *hortus* (garden), later converted to a second peristyle. The entrance on the left leads to the public area of the house through the massive double doors. On the mosaic 'doormat' is the Latin welcome, '*HAVE*'. The *fauces* (entrance hall) has two public *lararia* (household shrines) elaborately decorated in stucco high on the walls. The flooring comprises triangular pieces of coloured marble, a style known as *opus sectile*, originally embellished on the threshold to the *atrium* with a wonderful mosaic of actors' masks, garlands of flowers and fruit. This mosaic is now on display in the Naples Archaeological Museum. The front of the house is organised around two *atria* courtyards. On either side are small rooms, *cubicula*, used as guest

Above The remains of the magnificent Temple of Fortuna Augusta, situated on one of the most prominent cross-roads in Pompeii.

bedrooms or for private meetings with clients. On the far side is the *tablinum*, one of the most important rooms in the house, used by the seated patron for receiving clients and guests.

On either side of the *tablinum* there are two rooms, possibly used as winter and summer dining rooms. Walk through the *atrium* and you are in the first of the peristyles with a portico of 28 Ionic columns and a fountain and basin in the centre of the garden. The walls of the peristyle would have been covered with decorative stucco and paintings.

Opposite The doorway to the House of the Faun is framed by two elegant square Corinthian columns; it led to the atrium, the main public room.

Two highly decorated Corinthian columns frame the open room, or *exedra*, in the centre of the rear wall of the peristyle. The floor once held the famous Alexander mosaic now in the Naples Archaeological Museum along with mosaic scenes of the Nile from the threshold of the room. On either side of the Alexander mosaic room are two summer dining rooms facing into the wonderful garden of the second, larger peristyle with a Doric portico. On the far side of this more private peristyle garden is a small postern gate reserved exclusively for the use of the family. On the east side of the house is a service corridor isolating the kitchen, baths and slaves' quarters. It may be possible to identify the family who once lived in this great house. A statue base found during excavation has the Oscan name, V. Sadiriis, inscribed on it. The Latin form of the name is Satrius

The fabulous fourth-style paintings of cupid goldsmiths found in the large dining room (*triclinium*) of the House of the Vettii.

and the Greek name of Dionysus's companion is Satyros, who appears in a number of mosaics in the house. The placing of the statuette of the dancing satyr right in front of the *tablinum*, the most important room in the house, and displaying a satyr copulating with a maenad in the mosaic of the master bedroom would remind everyone of the semi-divine myth of the family's ancestors.

───────

HOUSE OF THE VETTII (VI.15.1)

When leaving the House of the Faun, turn left and left again down the narrow street Vicolo del Labirinto. If this street is closed, try the next turning on the left. When you reach the Vicolo di Mercurio, the House of the Vettii is in front of you. This house is of particular importance because of the survival of the rich fourth-style painting, as well as the sculpture and marble furnishings that were left *in situ* by the excavators, and not removed for the King of Naples to sell.

The rich brothers Aulus Vettius Restitutus and Aulus Vettius Conviva –

both freedmen – probably owned the house. Their names appear on nearby election notices and were carved into seals found close to the chests (*arcae*) located in the *atrium*. The house was planned to fit the restrictions of its position in the block and had four main architectural elements – the tuscanic *atrium*, the peristyle, the service *atrium* and a small private peristyle. A short service corridor on the south side ran between the *atrium* and a stable to a secondary entrance (no. 27).

On the east side of the main entrance there is a painting of Priapus, the god of fertility, with a very large phallus placed on one of the pans of a pair of scales, balanced on the other by a bag containing money. It probably served as a good luck talisman for health and prosperity. Below it a basket of fruit suggests the wealth of the Vettii brothers. On the other side of the entrance there is a painting of a sheep with the attributes of Mercury, the god of commerce. Both paintings promoted the wealth and health of the householders.

Beyond the entrance is the *atrium*, without the usual *tablinum*, however. This may suggest that although the Vettii brothers were obviously affluent, as freedmen they did not have clients calling in for the morning 'salutation' but rather went calling themselves. Alternatively the entire *atrium* with its two *alae* (adjoining rooms) could have been the venue for receiving clients. The *atrium* is decorated with magnificent fourth-style paintings and beyond, visible from the street through the open door, would be the peristyle with its *viridarium* (pleasure garden) and *trompe l'oeil* wall decoration on the far west wall. The wall decoration of the atrium is magnificent, with figures of children making sacrifices to the *penates* (household gods) against a black background. Above them the border is painted with winged cherubs active in scenes from the amphitheatre and circus. The *atrium* has been rebuilt and restored as far as the roof; the roof opening (*compluvium*) has its original terracotta lion's head waterspouts still in position

to pour rainwater into the pool below. Placed against the sidewalls on masonry bases, were two iron-covered strongboxes decorated with bronze studs. Two rooms (*cubicula*) flank the entrance hall (*vestibulum*); that on the left is painted in alternating red and white panels decorated with the scenes of Ariadne abandoned by Theseus, and of Hero and Leander. In the south-east corner, the reception room (*oecus*) is decorated with theatrical buildings painted on a white background and large yellow ochre panels have paintings that depict the myth of Cyparissus, Bacchus and Adriane watching the battle between Pan and Cupid. On the south side of the *atrium* is a long narrow hall that held the staircase to the upper floor and also gave access to a stable and the side entrance.

On the north-east side of the *atrium* is an opening to the smaller *atrium*, which is surrounded by the servants' quarters and dominated by a magnificent household shrine (*lararium*) dedicated to the gods of that particular

household. The household gods (*lares*) protected the household from external threats and are usually, as in the House of the Vettii, portrayed as two young men wearing short tunics, dancin, and holding drinking horns (rhytons) and dishes (paterae) in their hands. The styles of these domestic shrines vary from simple wall paintings to the type built at the House of the Vettii in the form of a small temple (*aedicula*), with the pediment supported by Corinthian columns. Between the paintings of the two *lares* is the genius that represents the head of the household (*paterfamilias*) making a sacrifice. Snakes were considered the guardian spirits of the family and they are shown underneath. Domestic rituals would be conducted at the *lararium* by the head of the household and would consist of daily prayers to the different household gods and regular small offerings of food from meals.

Next door to the *atrium* is the kitchen where the iron trivets, cooking pots and pans still sit where they were

found on the cinders of the range. Just off the kitchen is a small room, probably the household brothel, decorated with erotic scenes painted in a simple, direct style that leaves little to the imagination. Also displayed here is a statue of Priapus, which was found by the excavators in the kitchen. It probably belonged in the garden, however, as the statue could be used as a fountain with water jetting out of its huge penis. Priapus was a Greek god whose cult spread to Italy. Originally a god of fertility of crops and protection against harm, he later became primarily a god of gardens. His symbol was a phallus used as a protective charm against the evil eye. According to some myths, Priapus was the son of Dionysus (Bacchus) and was worshipped as part of the rites of Dionysus.

Retrace your steps into the main *atrium*. This leads into a magnificent peristyle with a central garden (*viridarium*) adorned with numerous small bronze and marble sculptures and benches. The garden would have been a haven of tranquillity with the sound of water cascading from fountains and splashing into basins. The running water was supplied via lead pipes, ultimately by Pompeii's aqueduct. Each fountain had its own bronze stopcock so that the display of water could be controlled and regulated.

Among the building's architectural novelties are two rooms facing the east portico of the peristyle. Both rooms originally had access to the peristyle and were decorated with wonderful fourth-style paintings derived from Greek mythological subject matter.

The two rooms were probably *exedrae*, imitating the picture galleries found in aristocratic palaces, where original and expensive works of art would be placed on view for guests.

The room to the north was possibly used as a dining room (*triclinium*) and is justly famous for the exquisite frieze of cherubs painted on to a black background. Starting from the left-hand door the scenes show: cherubs engaged in an archery competition, picking flowers and making garlands, making perfume, a chariot race, minting coins, baking bread, harvesting grapes, a festival in honour of Bacchus, and buying wine.

Next to the peristyle, and reached through a lockable door from the north wing, is a smaller, private peristyle located in the most secluded part of the house. It is decorated with erotic and feminine mythological subjects, including 'Achilles at Skyros discovered dressed as a woman among King Lycomedes' daughters' and 'Drunken Hercules surprising Augeus'. Although it has been suggested that the area was for the exclusive use of the owner's wife and daughters, as known from Greek houses, there is no evidence for that particular use in any other Roman house.

The House of the Vettii caused a sensation when excavated by Petra in 1894. The house and all its furnishing and works of art were almost intact and the decision, a controversial one, was to leave everything as found. It is one of the most frequently visited houses in Pompeii, and, unfortunately, has suffered serious damage to its

decorative surfaces by the thousands of visitors each year.

Turn left when you leave the front of the House of the Vettii and take the first right into the Vicolo dei Vettii and continue down Vicolo Storto to the Bakery of Popidius Priscus.

BAKERY OF POPIDIUS PRISCUS (VII.2.22)

The bakery adjoins the house of Popidius Priscus, a member of one of the most important families in Pompeii. About 35 bakeries have been found in Pompeii, each one with about four grindstones. This bakery follows a similar layout; a small service door connected the house and bakery. The main entrance to the bakery was on Vicolo Storto, but the bakery did not have a sales counter, suggesting deliveries were made to trade customers in the neighbourhood. The bakery used four large mills that stood outside in a row with room between them for the mules to turn the grindstones. The grindstone was carved out of a special type of lava rock quarried from the slopes of Mount Vesuvius. It was porous, but extremely hard, and very few fragments broke off during the grinding process. The base (*meta*) is cone-shaped and on it was placed a grindstone shaped as a hollow double truncated cone (*catillus*). The upper part of the *catillus* served as a funnel, into which the grain was poured, whilst the lower part ground the grain against the cone-shaped *meta*. The ground flour would filter down the sides of the *meta* to be collected in a collared tray (*lamina*) fitted around the base. To avoid excessive friction, a wooden beam that fitted the ear-lugs carved into the sides of the stone *catillus* could be used to lift it slightly from the *meta*. A blindfolded mule turned the whole contraption.

After grinding, the flour was sieved and water added to make dough. The dough could be mixed in an industrial-sized mixing machine equipped with paddles. Excavators discovered one such machine in the bakery. After being left to rest, the dough was wrapped in a cloth and put in a kneading trough located on a masonry bench on the south side of the bakery. Here it was shaped into round loaves, divided into eight portions with a double cross, and stamped with the baker's seal.

The oven, which had a large polygonal combustion chamber, was filled with vine faggots and lit. The smoke went out of a long flue at the front. The fire was kept alight until the bricks of the vault became white-hot. It would have taken about an hour and a half to heat the oven. Then the bread was put into the oven with a wooden paddle and the oven closed with an iron shutter fitted with a sliding panel to regulate the heat. It would have taken about 30–45 minutes to bake the bread. Halfway through the baking process the loaves would have been coated with water using a mop to give them a shiny surface. At the Modestus Bakery (VII.1.36), excavators found 81 somewhat overcooked loaves in the oven, indicating the scale of bread production at Pompeii.

On leaving the bakery, turn left down the Vicolo Storto, and left again into the Via degli Augustali to continue

the tour, or right for lunch at the café behind the souvenir shop. Take the first turning on the right along the Via degli Augustali. This is the Vicolo del Lupanare and it leads to the Brothel.

BROTHEL (VII.12.18)

Called the *lupanar* (the Latin *lupa* means both she-wolf and prostitute), the brothel seems to have been run by two men called Victor and Africanus. Over 30 brothels have been found in Pompeii ranging from a single room with a straw mattress to superior establishments attached to bath-houses. On the ground floor of this establishment there are five rooms opening off a through-corridor that has entrances at 18 Vicolo del Lupanare and 19 Vicolo del Balcone Pensile. There is a small latrine in the west corner and five more rooms upstairs. The rooms are simply furnished with a masonry bed-base and painted white. They are covered with graffiti left by the clients who proclaim the virtues and vices of incumbent prostitutes. Above the doors leading

The four large mills of the bakery probably stood outside and were turned by mules. The large oven would take 30–45 minutes to bake the bread.

into the rooms are paintings illustrating scenes of the 'speciality' of the house. On the opposite wall is a painting of the Greek god Priapus in front of a fig tree holding the testicles of a double phallus in each hand.

Prostitution, although rife in Pompeii, was considered disgraceful and the respectable upper classes would have nothing to do with it. No doubt they had favoured slave girls and boys at their beck and call instead. The cost to the brothel client was low, ranging from two to six *asses*, enough to buy a couple of glasses of good wine. Prostitutes had to be registered with the city authorities and were barred from holding public office.

Leaving the brothel, turn right into the Vicolo del Lupanare and the Stabian Baths are on your left.

STABIAN BATHS (VII.1.8)

Excavated between 1853 and 1858 by Ruggiero, the Stabian Bath complex had been pillaged after the eruption of AD 79 by gangs of Romans looking for expensive marble statues and furnishings. The interior has been fully described on page 135. Established in the second century BC, it was enlarged in the years immediately following the arrival of Sulla's veterans in 80 BC. The bathing suites occupy the east wing of the building. The furnace room separated men and women from each other. The centre of the bath complex is occupied by an exercise yard surrounded on three sides by a colonnaded portico. Public latrines are found in the north wing, whilst on the west side is the swimming pool. The sequence of bathing rooms, for both men and women, is typical of this type of establishment. From the vestibule, off which was the cold plunge-bath (*frigidarium*), one entered the changing room (*apodyterium*), then the warm room (*tepidarium*) and finally the hot room (*caldarium*).

Turn left when you leave the baths, then right into the Via Stabiana, which will lead you to the Theatre District.

A painting of the Theatre District of Pompeii. The Triangular Forum is to the left, whilst the gladiators' barracks are in front of the large theatre.

THEATRE DISTRICT

Turn right into the Via del Tempio d'Iside and walk past the theatres on your left. Ahead at the end of the road is the Triangular Forum. This spot is one of the most beautiful in Pompeii. It is situated on top of a ridge of lava that overlooks the Sarnus Valley and the Bay of Naples. Occupied from the sixth century BC, when a wonderful

Doric temple of Greek or Etruscan origin was constructed here, the land was sacred and the sanctuary was separate from the early town of Pompeii that was developing around the Temple of Apollo and the adjacent market.

Access to the Triangular Forum is near the crossroads through a monumental entrance (*propylaeum*) originally comprising six tall, elegant Ionic columns. After the excavation in the eighteenth century, three columns and one semi-column were restored. Walk through the left side of the entrance and ahead of you is the great three-sided portico that delineated the sacred area. Originally there were about 100 columns and a number have been restored on the east side in front of the

The fountain and a marble-faced base for a statue of Marcellus, situated just inside the entrance to the Triangular Forum.

rear exterior of the theatre. Near the entrance stand a fountain and a marble-faced base for a statue dedicated to Marcellus, a nephew of Augustus. For a short time prior to his early death he held the office of *patronus* of Pompeii, an honorific title given in the hope of favour at the imperial court.

It has been suggested, quite convincingly, that the eastern portico, which is the longest side of the Triangular Forum, was used as an open-air and covered racetrack (*xystus*). Although only half a *stadium* in length (a *stadium* is 120 metres/393 feet), it could have been used for athletic and horse races held as part of the religious festivals associated with the Doric temple in the south-west of the Triangular Forum. The Doric temple dates back to the middle of the sixth century BC and was rebuilt a number of times between the fifth and second centuries BC. It has an unusual south-east

orientation, probably so that ships arriving at the mouth of the River Sarno could see it. Its ground plan is unclear, but it is likely that it was completely colonnaded and planned as a typical Greek temple. The surviving altar is on the south-east side, which suggests there should be another similar altar on the west side. The two altars would have been dedicated to two deities, probably Minerva and Hercules, as portrayed on the roof ornaments (*antefixae*) recovered by the excavators. Further evidence is found in an incomplete Oscan inscription painted on a nearby tuff pillar. The Doric temple was probably a picturesque ruin at the time of the AD 79 volcanic eruption, and had been for many years. Around the temple are a number of other interesting monuments. At the temple's north-west corner is a semi-circular seat with ends carved with winged lion's paws. Its Latin inscription tells us that the *duoviri* Lucius Sepunius Sandilianus and Marcus Herennius Epidianus dedicated the seat – called a *schola*.

A small temple stands near the foot of the steps leading up to the front of the main temple. It could be the symbolic tomb (*heroon*) of the mythical founder of the city. In front of the temple is a round shrine (*tholos*) with seven Doric columns (four still stand) that surround an older sacred well. The function of the well is not known; it could be for sacred water or, being near the possible tomb of the founder of the city, the shrine was perhaps a meeting place betweem the world of the living and the netherworld of the dead (*mundus*). Elaborate rites were

closely connected with such structures preceding the foundation of a city.

Walk back to the entrance to the Triangular Forum and, facing the Via del Tempio d'Iside, the Samnite Gymnasium will be on your right.

SAMNITE GYMNASIUM

With the rebuilding of parts of the Triangular Forum in the second century BC, a building known as the Samnite Gymnasium was constructed, comprising a porticoed courtyard built with slender Doric columns. The east side of the portico was demolished when the adjacent Temple of Isis was rebuilt following the earthquake of AD 62. Located in the courtyard in front of the main entrance is a stone flight of stairs and a base that probably held a statue of Hermes, the Greek messenger god who was the protector of athletes. It was customary to put the laurel crown intended for the winners on top of the platform. The winning athlete would then ascend the stairs, collect the crown and consecrate his victory by placing the crown on the head of Hermes. The rooms located in the western part of the gymnasium were used for various athletic activities. One of the most famous statues excavated at Pompeii was found nearby in 1797. It is among the most complete marble copies of the *Doryphorus* (Lance-bearer) of Polyclitus, whose bronze original was made by the famous Greek sculptor in about 440 BC.

Adjacent to the gymnasium on the east side is the Temple of Isis.

TEMPLE OF ISIS

The sanctuary around the Temple of Isis (page 46) is enclosed by walls on its east and north sides. It adjoins the Samnite Gymnasium to the west and the theatres to the south. Very little is

The Temple of Isis standing on a high platform reached by a stone staircase. To the left is the customary altar placed outside temple buildings.

left of the original temple because it had been almost completely destroyed by the earthquake of AD 62. It was completely rebuilt in interesting circumstances by Numerius Popidius Celsinus. He was a six-year-old child who was admitted into the ruling body of Pompeii, the *collegium decurionum*, as a reward for his generosity (his father having actually provided the finances).

The discovery and excavation in the eighteenth century by I a Vega of this small, but wonderfully decorated, temple created a sensation and it became a 'must-see' for foreigners on the Grand Tour. The temple stands on a high platform (*podium*) reached by a stone staircase at the front. It had four Corinthian columns in front (*pronaos*) of the shrine (*cella*). The inside of the shrine was decorated with white stucco and against the back wall is a platform with bases for the cult statues of Isis and Osiris. The platform is hollow, as it was used to store the cult regalia and instruments. There is a small door and an external staircase on the south side, possibly to allow priests to enter the shrine quietly during ceremonies. On either side of the main entrance are two niches. One was probably for a statue of Harpocrates, the Egyptian deity Horus who was the son of Isis. The other statue was probably Anubis, the jackal-headed Egyptian god of the dead (usually portrayed on Roman statues with a dog's head). The façade of the shrine was lavishly decorated with Corinthian pilasters supporting small pediments rendered in stucco. A statue of Dionysus dedicated by

Numerius Popidius Ampliatus, the father of the six-year-old boy who rebuilt the temple, was found in a niche on the back wall.

The customary altar in front of the temple is situated to the left so as not to impede processions to and from the temple. Excavators in the eighteenth century claimed to have found 'the ashes and burnt bones of the victims still on top of the altar'. Just beside the altar is a basement shrine (*purgatorium*) in which sacred water from the Nile was stored. West of the courtyard is a great hall with five arched entrances that has been identified as a *telesterion*, a room for the performing of sacred dramas, an area for the holding of ritual banquets and a meeting hall. The paintings, mostly removed to the Naples Archaeological Museum, show landscapes of Upper and Lower Egypt and scenes of the myth of Io and her arrival in Egypt. The priests lived on the south side of the courtyard, where various rooms including a bedroom, dining room and kitchen have been identified. Nearly everything found in the temple, including ornaments, the statues of Isis and Dionysus, and almost all the paintings, have been removed and are now on display in a wing of the Naples Archaeological Museum dedicated to Isis.

To the east and adjacent to the temple of Isis is the Temple of Jupiter Meilichios.

TEMPLE OF JUPITER MEILICHIOS

The temple was built in the second century BC. Eighteenth-century excavators found a terracotta statue and two busts in the ruins, and the

identification of the deity has since then been questioned. At the end of the nineteenth century, August Mau suggested the building was dedicated to Jupiter Meilichios, the identification based on a pre-Roman Oscan inscription found at the site. Jupiter Meilichios is the Roman version of Zeus Meilichios, a cult favoured by the Greeks in Sicily but rare amongst the Romans. The deity was the patron of farmers and was especially associated with agriculture and abundant crops. The temple itself is modest and seems to have been used as a temporary place of worship for the Capitoline triad of Jupiter, Minerva and Juno when their temple was destroyed in the earthquake of AD 62.

Leaving the temple, turn right towards the Stabian Gate and on your right is a passage leading to the Theatres.

THEATRES

The large theatre, the small theatre (*odeion*) and the gladiators' barracks (*porticus post scaenam*) all constitute a unified architectural complex built to Greek ideals in the second century BC. The present appearance of the large theatre (page 178) is a result of the renovations carried out to the building during the reign of Augustus and restorations undertaken after the earthquake of AD 62. The theatre was built against the natural slope of the hill, which made construction easier. The renovation work during the Augustan period was supervised by the architect Marcus Artorius Primus, a former slave, and sponsored by Marcus Holconius Rufus and Marcus

Holconius Celer, members of one of the more prominent families in Pompeii whose wealth came from the production and sale of wine.

The theatre was divided into three distinct zones, the *ima cavea* (closest to the stage), the *media cavea* (from where one had the best view of the stage) and the *summa cavea* (up in the 'gods'). They in their turn were sub-divided into five sections by six vertical passageways. The *ima cavea*, reserved for members of the local senate, consisted of four rows of seats. The *media cavea* had 20 rows of seats, and the *summa cavea*, of which little survives, probably had four rows of seats.

Above The large theatre showing the seats divided into three zones and five sections.

Right The sculptures of kneeling *telamone* figures support the stone shelf on the outer wall of the seating area in the *odeion*.

Between the *ima cavea* and the stage is the horseshoe-shaped orchestra pit where the musicians used to sit. In the same area were the *critici*, sitting on folding chairs, who would pass comments on the performances. The front of the stage (*proscaenium*) had steps that were used by the actors if they wished to

take the play off the stage and into the audience.

The narrow groove in the walls at the back of the stage is for the interval curtain. At the back of the stage stands the backdrop (*frons scaenae*). Its structure dates from the reconstruction after the earthquake of AD 62 when it was probably raised to two storeys, reproducing the façade of an aristocratic palace. Actors coming from backstage, where the dressing rooms were situated, could use three doors. Two highly decorated boxes, one either side of the stage, gave an elevated view and were reserved for the city's VIPs.

The small theatre or *odeion* is located to the east of the large theatre. Built by Caius Quintus Valgus and Marcus Porcius, the *odeion* (page 40) is a roofed building that mimics many of the forms of the large theatre. It has been suggested that the *odeion* may have been used as a meeting place for Sulla's Roman veterans. However, given that the building is described in contemporary inscriptions as a roofed theatre (*theatrum tectum*), the architectural layout and attention to the acoustics suggest the building was used for poetic recitals, music, singing and mime shows. Whereas the capacity of the large theatre was around 5,000, the *odeion* could seat only about 1,000 spectators.

Behind the large theatre are the gladiators' barracks, arranged as a large four-sided portico surrounded by 74 Doric columns. The building dates from the second century BC and was originally used by the spectators of the two theatres during the inter-vals. During this period, the porticoes probably enclosed an ornate public garden embellished with statues and fountains. Following the earthquake of AD 62, the access gates to the theatres were walled up and the area was rebuilt as gladiators' barracks (*ludus*). In one of the rooms, two wooden boxes full of gladiators' weapons wrapped in fine cloth were found. More gruesome discoveries were 22 victims of the eruption of AD 79; the excavators found all the bodies in one room, including a woman adorned with magnificent gold jewellery.

On leaving the theatre district, walk back into the city and turn right into the Via dell'Abbondanza, one of the main roads of Pompeii. Named after the relief on the fountain near the forum that portrays the goddess of abundance as a young woman holding a horn of plenty (*cornucopia*), the street was lined with shops (*tabernae*), inns where hot meals were served (*cauponae*) and cafés where hot and cold food was sold (*thermopolia*). It was Pompeii's main commercial street in the first century AD, and was once lined with grand mansions. However, the emergence of affluent freedmen and the need of some penniless aristocrats to rent out rooms in their fine houses changed the character of the street. The front rooms of mansions were taken over by shops and bars. During the last years of the city this street bustled with activity, with crowds buying and selling, drinking and eating, as they promenaded from the civic forum to the amphitheatre.

Join this street of ghosts and walk towards the amphitheatre on the east side of the city. On your right, just past the Vicolo del Citarista, is the Fullery of Stephanus.

FULLERY OF STEPHANUS (I.6.7)

The building was excavated by Spinazzola in 1913, and was named after two graffiti found painted on the façade of the building: 'Stephanus recommends' and 'all fullers recommended'. The fullery is one of the largest in Pompeii, which had about 17 such establishments. The house that originally occupied this site was probably restored after the earthquake of AD 62, but then sold to Stephanus who converted the building into a fullery. The laundering facilities were situated on the ground floor with living quarters upstairs.

The entrance door, which is wider than usual probably to allow customers easy access, was found locked and barred by the excavators. Behind the door were a number of bodies, one of which was clutching a bag of gold and silver coins amounting to 1,090 *sesterces* – probably the day's takings. To the right of the entrance is a small room, probably used as a reception area, where clothes could be handed in or collected and payments made. The washing area was located at the rear of the building in the peristyle and courtyard area. Three inter-connecting vats were found on descending levels, along with five oval basins. The woven cloth was scoured in these basins using a mixture of water and soda or other alkaline agents such as human urine. The cloth was also treated with 'fuller's earth', which strengthened it before it was transferred to the large tanks for beating, washing and rinsing. The next important step was 'carding', which removed fibres that were tangled on the surface of the cloth, and 'sulphurisation', in which a solution of sulphur steam gave the cloth a sheen. After the last wash in the large tank that Stephanus had constructed in the *atrium* in place of the *impluvium*, there was a final finishing such as sizing, brushing and trimming. The finished cloth was dried on the terrace constructed above the pitched roof of the *atrium* and ironed in the press, worked by two large screws, which stood in the entrance on the left. Outside the entrance, Stephanus had permission from the magistrates to dry clothes alongside the road if need be.

On leaving the laundry, turn right towards the amphitheatre and walk for two blocks. On the corner, on your right, is a typical *thermopolium*.

THERMOPOLIUM OF VETUTIUS PLACIDUS (I.8.8)

Usually located on a main street, a *thermopolium* was a place where hot and cold food and wine was sold. It consisted of an L-shaped masonry counter which contained large terracotta pots (*dolia*) to hold the food, which were sunk down. Sometimes customers could eat sitting down in rooms located behind the bar. The bar was usually equipped with cauldrons and ovens to prepare snacks quickly for those in a hurry to catch a show at the amphitheatre. The same kind of scenario can be seen on the streets of Naples today at numerous fast-service pizzerias and cafés.

This particular bar is thought to have belonged to Vetutius Placidus, as graffiti on the front wall says that he owned the house next door. The household shrine (*lararium*) on the back wall is typical in that it portrays the customary household gods in the act of sacrifice, but also includes Dionysus, the god of wine, and Mercury, the god of commerce. Underneath, two snakes are sacrificed at an altar. Snakes (or serpents) in pagan religions possessed healing powers and they were considered as *genii* (guardian spirits) of the god Agathos Daimon. They were also considered to be messengers of the gods, because of their ability to disappear into the ground (the underworld). The shedding of their skin led to snakes becoming a powerful symbol of eternal rebirth, rejuvenation and renewed health. With the coming of Christianity snakes were recast as demons of evil.

Continue along the Via dell'Abbondanza for six blocks and next door to

The bar of Vetutius Placidus. The large terracotta pots sunk into the counter were used to hold hot food. The household shrine can be seen on the back wall.

the Vicolo di Octavius Quartio is the House of Loreius Tiburtinus.

HOUSE OF LOREIUS TIBURTINUS (II.2.2)

The house was excavated by Spinazzola from 1916 to 1921, who named it after the numerous election graffiti found on the front of the house and on the houses opposite. Further evidence can be found in the house itself, where under a painting of a priest of Isis is written 'Amulius Faventinus Tiburs'. The last owner was probably Octavius Quartio, whose inscribed signet ring was found on the floor of the room to the right of the entrance. He seems to be the person who converted the house for the domestic worship of Isis. The frontage of the house has a number of inns (cauponae) built into it and probably let out by Quartio.

Walk through the entrance and you enter the *atrium* with the usual rooms off it. Ahead of you should be the most important room in the house, the *tablinum*, where Octavius Quartio received his clients. This area was rebuilt following the devastation of the AD 62 earthquake. The *tablinum* and the adjoining dining room were removed and the garden considerably enlarged. In fact, the garden is one of the most important features of the house. Where the *tablinum* stood is now the pleasure garden (*viridarium*) enclosed by a small peristyle. Two of the most exciting painted rooms are situated here. On your far right a small dining room (*oecus*) is decorated in fourth style with elegant white panels divided by architectural details and miniature decorations. The ceiling, part of which has survived, is decorated with circular and square partitions that contain wonderful stucco reliefs. The most interesting painting is the portrait of a priest of Isis; bald-headed and dressed in a white garment he holds a rattle (*sistrum*) in his right hand, the instrument frequently used in the ceremonies of the goddess Isis. The other dining room (*triclinium*), almost opposite and at the head of the water canals, contains paintings that depict Hercules' battle with Laomedon, King of Troy, whilst the lower pictures show scenes from the Trojan War featuring Achilles.

Step outside the room and you can see a most wonderful formal garden constructed around a whole series of ornamental pools (*euripi*). These long, narrow, rectangular pools are usually seen in much larger gardens. A pergola, supported on pillars once decorated with Bacchic scenes and surrounded by many garden statues, covers the upper pool. The house wall is painted with a large hunting scene, whilst other walls show the myths of Diana and Actaeon and of Narcissus and Pyramus. The only painter's signature found in Pompeii appears here – *Lucius pinxit*. The lower pool, set at right angles to the upper pool, runs through the large garden, which has been planted with fruit trees and acanthus plants. On either side are pergola-covered walkways. Where the two pools interconnect stands a third-style shrine equipped with a fountain in the centre and ringed by a semi-circle of inclined water jets with a vertical jet in the centre. Another shrine (*aedicula*) is situated at the far end of the lower pool, whilst halfway along was a very unusual cascade fountain built in white marble as a kind of stepped pyramid which the water would have tinkled down.

The upper pool terminated on the east side in a splendid summer dining room (*triclinium aestivum*), which was ideally placed to enjoy the late afternoon sun and dine *al fresco*. The dining couches would have been separated by a miniature shrine, which contained a statue of a crouching young man pouring water from an amphora. The paintings on either side depict the myth of Narcissus and the one on the right the myth of Pyramus and Thisbe, the former killing himself in the belief that a lion had devoured his lover. On coming across his dead body, Thisbe committed suicide.

On leaving the house, turn right and next door is the House of Venus in the Sea-Shell.

HOUSE OF VENUS IN THE SEA SHELL (II.3.3)

This house, excavated by Maiuri in 1952, is named after the wonderful painting on the back wall of the peristyle. It portrays Venus lying in a sea-shell with her cloak acting as a sail or sunshade, accompanied by a cupid astride a dolphin, whilst another cupid looks on. This house, like the previous dwelling, seems to have been adapted from an *atrium* house in which the *tablinum* was removed to give more room for the peristyle. The dining room is large and spacious and opens out into both the *atrium* and peristyle with wonderful views of the formal garden, and the famous painting of Venus. To the right of the Venus painting is a painting portraying a marble statue of Mars separated from a *trompe l'oeil* garden by a trellised fence.

On leaving the house, turn right and right again, and at the bottom of the lane you will see the amphitheatre (page 183) on your left and the *palaestra* (page 181) on your right.

PALAESTRA

Also known as the large gymnasium, the *palaestra* was built at the time of Augustus as a place to practise gymnastics and athletics. It was also used for many other activities, including slave auctions and cock-fights, and as a military camp. The area is surrounded by a *triporticus* built of 100 Ionic-Corinthian columns. The portico was

lined with two rows of shady plane trees, the roots of which were reproduced in plaster casts by the excavators. In the centre was a very large swimming pool and the overflow channel from the pool flushed the latrines situated on the southern side. Along the longest side of the arcade there was a rectangular room, probably dedicated to the imperial cult.

AMPHITHEATRE

The amphitheatre is one of the few monuments at Pompeii to have remained partially exposed throughout the Middle Ages and it is the earliest building that we know was used for gladiatorial games. Built by the magistrates Caius Quinctius Valgus and Marcus Porcius in around 70 BC, the building was originally called a *spectacula*, which literally means 'a building for spectacles'. The amphitheatre could seat about 20,000 spectators who would travel from far and wide to see the spectacles. Situated in the south-east corner of Pompeii, away from the civic forum, two gates – the Sarno and Nuceria – served it, and the city authorities could control the crowds in this confined area.

The arena is lower than the surrounding area; the excavated earth was banked up as a base for the tiers of seats and the bank of the city wall was used for the same purpose.

The tombs outside the Nuceria Gate form an extraordinary group of about fifty tombs of differing architectural styles from the most humble to the most extravagant.

To reach their seats, spectators could use any of the six external staircases. Privileged citizens had two choices, either to use one of the two street-level corridors or to use the same entrance as the gladiators. Along the minor axis of the amphitheatre is an additional passage connecting the arena to the outside. The small door opening on to the arena is called the *porta libitinensis* after the Roman goddess Libitina, who supervised funerals and rites in honour of the dead. It is thought that the dead bodies of gladiators were removed from the arena through this door and passageway. The elliptic arena was surrounded by a 1.8-metre (6-foot) parapet topped by a metal fence as protection for the crowd. The parapet was originally decorated with wonderful pictures of gladiatorial combat. These no longer exist but were copied by nineteenth-century artists.

The city authorities quickly restored the amphitheatre after it was damaged in the earthquake of AD 62, no doubt as a palimpsest against the difficult and troubled times facing the city as it strove to repair the damage caused by the earthquake.

Walk towards the Nuceria Gate, and beyond is part of Pompeii's city of the dead.

NUCERIA GATE NECROPOLIS

The Romans buried their dead by inhumation or cremation and occasionally by embalming. Cremation was the dominant rite in Pompeii, with the burial of the ashes in a tomb to shield the dead from the view of the gods of whom the deceased had no further

need. The deceased was laid to rest, wearing a toga, on a litter or couch and, if he were a magistrate, bearing his badges of office. The funeral procession would pass through the town to the place of cremation, where he was burnt on a pyre and his ashes gathered and placed in a glass or terracotta urn. If glass, it was usually put inside a lead container. The container was then deposited in the sacred enclosure of the tomb and a bust erected to mark the spot. The busts, if made of marble, usually bear a short inscription indicating the name and age of the deceased. Each year, the Festival of the Dead (*Feralia*) was celebrated for nine days, ending on 21 February. This was when the family would perform rites at the tomb to commemorate the deceased. Private ceremonies (*Parentalia*) were also carried out on the anniversary of their death.

Burials had to be outside the *pomerium* (sacred public land) of the town according to Roman law. This law was enforced at Pompeii, for outside the Nuceria Gate stands a stone pillar stating: 'Suedius Clemens, Emperor Vespasian's envoy to Pompeii, after investigating and taking appropriate measures, restored the public land unlawfully occupied by private individuals to the town of Pompeii.' Buildings were razed to the ground in the vicinity of the pillar, and tombs built on the *pomerium* were destroyed.

There is an extraordinary group of almost 50 tombs, lining both sides of the road that runs parallel to the walls outside the Nuceria Gate. Excavated first in 1886–7 and then again in the

1950s by Maiuri, the great twentieth-century archaeologist, the group is characterised by the customary mixing of tombs of different social and architectural types. Maiuri found the sight of numerous corpses along the road of Pompeians who had been fleeing from the volcanic eruption of AD 79 so heart-breaking that at times it was difficult for him to continue working.

The dead of some of the leading families of Pompeii are buried here, the Sepunii, Epidii, Tillii, Octavii, Caesii, Stronnii. One of the tombs identified included an enclosure tomb with a pediment façade. Dated to the time of Nero (AD 54–68), it contains the remains of Gaius Munatius Faustus and his wife Naevoleia Tyche. Next to it is a tomb of the late republic (second

to first century BC). It is fronted by an archway flanked by three niches on each side, surmounted by a second level with eight more niches. In two of them tuff busts of a male and female are displayed identified by inscriptions as Publius Flavius Philoxenos and Flavia Agathea. The next tomb is the large central tomb erected during the time of Tiberius (AD 14–37) by Eumachia, the priestess of Venus, for herself and her family. It is one of the most impressive tombs found at Pompeii for the woman who erected the large building named after her in the forum. The next tomb dates from the late republic (second to first century AD) and it consists of a high podium supporting a shrine built as a temple with four columns (prostyle

tetrastyle). The columns frame three niches with an armed young man between his two parents. The accompanying inscription has the names of those buried, Marcus Octavius and his wife Vertia Philumena.

The last tomb of some interest is an Augustan *aedicula*-style tomb standing on a high podium and containing three figures. The statue of the deceased freedman Publius Vesonius Phileros is on the left; in the centre is his patroness Vesonia, and on the right his friend Marcus Ortellius Faustus, also a freedman. The inscription with the latter tells us: 'Oh passer-by, stop for a short while, if you do not mind, and learn what you should be wary of. One whom I hoped was my friend accused me falsely. In the court, by grace of the gods and due to my innocence, I was absolved from all accusations. May the slanderer be rejected by the Gods of the Household [*Penates*] and the gods of the Beyond.'

This is a unique insight into a world that stopped on 24 August AD 79, and the bitter reflections of Publius Vesonius Phileros will forever echo through time.

Walk back towards the Nuceria Gate where the itinerary ends – you can exit the site here, or you can make your own way back to the Marine Gate entrance and savour the atmosphere of Pompeii.

Looking back from the tombs outside the walls of Pompeii towards the Nucerian Gate. In the distance is Vesuvius, the sleeping giant of Campania.

ACKNOWLEDGEMENTS

I wish to thank the following:
All the excavators of Pompeii, past and present, and especially J. B. Ward-Perkins who was my inspiration and mentor during those hot dusty days excavating in Campania so long ago. To Sophie Wallace-Hadrill and Helena Caldon who provided excellent support and inspiration and to Ernest Black, Louise Tucker, Tracey White and last but not least to Daisy, my constant feline companion who died the day the book was started.

BBC Worldwide would like to thank the following for providing photographs and for permission to reproduce copyright material. While every effort has been made to trace and acknowledge copyright holders, we would like to apologize should there have been any errors or omissions.

All photographs in this book have been provided by Alfredo and Pio Foglia with the exception of the following:
AKG London: pp. 57, 78, 100; Alinari/Roger Viollet: p. 93; The Art Archive: pp. 35, 48, 66 (below), 128, 154, 174; Bridgeman Art Library: pp. 5c, 27, 31, 52-3, 61 (above), 63; Sonia Halliday: pp. 54, 69; The Louvre/RMN: pp. 81, 84, 156; National Trust Photo Library: pp. 5a, 7; Scala: pp. 10, 147; Roger Viollet: pp. 89, 151; Werner Forman Archive: pp. 19, 21, 25, 184.

BBC Books would also like to thank the following for permission to reproduce text from their publications:

Dover publications for extracts from Vitruvius, *Ten Books of Architecture*, translated by Morris Hicky Morgan, 1960.
Loeb Classical Library: Seneca, *Vols VII and X, Naturales Questiones*, Trans. T. H. Corcoran, Cambridge, Mass: Harvard University Press, 1971. Livy, *The History of Rome*, Trans. Evan T. Sage. Cambridge, Mass: Harvard University Press. Martial, *Epigrams*, Trans. D. R. Shackleton Bailey, Cambridge, Mass: Harvard University Press, 1969. The Loeb Classical Library ® is a registered trademark of the President and Fellows of Harvard College. Penguin books for Pliny, *Letters of the Younger Pliny*, Trans. B. Radice 1963, Penguin Classics 1969; Juvenal, *The Sixteen Satires*, Trans. P. Green, Penguin 1967. Harper Collins Publishers Ltd. for Goethe, *Italian Journey*, © 1962 translated by W. H. Auden. Copyright in the customised version vests in BBC.

GLOSSARY

Ala Side passages to the left and right of the far end of the atrium in a Roman house. Perhaps used as offices or waiting rooms or to let light into the atrium.

Ambulatio A terrace for exercise and walking.

Apodyterium Changing room of a bath building. Usually furnished with long benches along the walls and recesses in the walls for clothes.

Ashlar Masonry of regular squared stones laid in horizontal courses with vertical joints.

Atlantes Carved male figures serving as pillars. Also called *telamones.*

Atriolum Small atrium or hall.

Atrium The central area of the front part of a Republican Roman house. Bedrooms (see *cubicula*) were situated here. The central part of the roof, (*compluvium*) or rain collector, sloped inwards to a central *impluvium* or catch basin, which supplied water to the storage tanks beneath the ornamental pond.

Basilica An oblong rectangular building with a central nave and two side aisles lit by clerestory windows. Used for commercial and legal purposes, and later in the Christian period as the blueprint for early churches.

Caementa Irregular pieces of stone or brick used as aggregate in Roman concrete, ie, *opus caementicium.*

Caldarium The hot or steam room of Roman baths.

Cardo Roman surveying term for north–south streets in Roman towns.

Cella Usually the room of a temple which contained the statue of the divinity.

Columbarium Dovecote, but also used to describe a sepulchral chamber containing cremation urns.

Cryptoporticus Underground, vaulted colonnade or portico with lighting through the vault or side walls.

Cubiculum Guest bedrooms situated around the *atrium.*

Decumanus Roman surveying term for east–west streets in Roman towns.

Domus An elegant Roman house for a single family, usually single-storyed with rooms facing onto the *atrium* and onto a porticoed garden.

Exedra Semi-circular or rectangular recess with an open front, sometimes a semi-circular-stone bench.

Fauces Entrance hall to the *atrium.*

Frigidarium Cold room in the Roman baths.

Horrea Large warehouses used for the storage of food and grain.

Hortus Garden or park.

Hypocaust Floors suspended on brick piers to allow hot air from a furnace to circulate and heat the rooms.

Insula Usually an apartment house, but also used to denote a city block.

Lararium A shrine for the household gods located inside the Roman house or garden.

Laconicum A small circular sauna or sweat room in the Roman baths.

Natatio The large swimming pool at Roman baths.

Nymphaeum Originally a cave with running water and sacred to nymphs. Later an artificial grotto with fountains.

Oecus A type of living or reception room, in the Roman house .

Oscillum A small, circular marble disc carved with the faces of deities and hung from trees in the garden to tinkle in the wind.

Palaestra Exercise ground used for wrestling, athletics and ball games.

Peristyle Colonnaded, inner-garden courtyard in Pompeian houses.

Piscina Occasionally a fish pond but more usually plunge pools in Roman baths.

Popina A tavern or inn where meals were sold.

Quadriporticus Enclosed courtyard with porticoes on all four sides.

Socle The lower part of a Roman wall.

Taberna A room used as a inn or a shop opening off from the street.

Tablinum The main room in a Roman house situated between the *atrium* and inner peristyle, originally the master bedroom, later used as the office by the head of the household.

Tepidarium Warm room of a Roman bath.

Thermae Large public baths found throughout the Roman Empire.

Thermopolium A Roman restaurant where hot food and drinks are sold.

Triclinium Usually a dining-room with three banqueting couches, found in Roman houses.

Velarium A cloth awning stretched over the theatre or amphitheatre as protection against the sun.

Viridarium A Roman pleasure garden.

BIBLIOGRAPHY

Wheeler R.E.M. (1964)
Roman Art and Architecture (London)

Toynbee J.M.C. (1965)
The Art of the Romans (London)

Picard G. (1970)
Roman Painting (London)

Mairui A. (1963)
Herculaneum and the Villa of the Papyri
(Novara)

Boethius A. and Ward-Perkins J.B.
(1970)
Etruscan and Roman Architecture (London)

Brion M. (1960)
*Pompeii and Herculaneum: The Glory and
the Grief* (London)

Sir Banister Fletcher (1956)
*A History of Architecture on the
Comparative Method* (London)

Capasso, Gaetano (2002)
*Journey to Pompeii – Virtual Tours around
the Lost Cities* (Capware)

Mau A. (1902)
Pompeii: Its Life and Art
Trans. F.W. Kelsey (Berlin)

McKay A.G. (1975)
*Houses, Villas and Palaces in the Roman
World* (London)

Gardner J.F. (1986)
Women in Roman Law and Society
(London)

Friedlander L (1908)
*Roman Life and Manners under the Early
Empire 4 vols.*
Trans. L.A. Magnus and J.H. Freese
(London)

Zevi F. (1979)
*Pompeii 79: Raccolta di studiper il
decimonono centenario dell'eruzione
vesuviana* (Naples)

Ward-Perkins J.B. (1979)
*Note di topografia e urbanistica, in Zevi
(1979)*

Wallace-Hadrill A. (1994)
*Houses and Society in Pompeii and
Herculaneum* (Princetown)

Laurence R. (1994)
Roman Pompeii: Space and Society
(London)

Clarke W.B. (1830)
Pompeii: Its Past and Present State
(London)

Carrington J.C. (1933)
*Notes on the Building Materials of
Pompeii* (Journal of Roman Studies,
London)

Moreno Paolo (2001)
Apelles The Alexander Mosaic (Skira)

Filippo Coarelli (Ed.) (2002)
Pompeii (Riverside Book Company)

Colin Amery and Brian Curran J.R.
(2002)
The Lost World of Pompeii
(Francis Lincoln Ltd)

Robert Etienne (1998)
Pompeii – The Day a City Died.
(New Horizon/Thames and Hudson).

Pier Giovanni Guzzo and Antonio
d'Ambrosio (2002)
Pompeii, Guide to the Site. UK edition.
(Electa Napoli)

Salvatore Nappo (1998)
Pompeii (Wiedenfeld and Nicolson)

Jerome Carcopino (1991)
Daily Life in Ancient Rome (Penguin)

Karl Christ (1984)
The Romans
(University of California Press)

Sara E. Bon and Rick Jones (Eds.)
(1997)
Sequence and Space in Pompeii
(Oxbow Books)

Roger Ling (1997)
*The Insula of the Menander at Pompeii –
Volume 1: The Structures*
(Clarenden Press)

Paul Zanker (2000)
Pompeii. Public and Private Life (Harvard)

Antonio d'Ambrosio (1998)
Discovering Pompeii (Electa)

Antonio d'Ambrosio (1998)
Unpeeling Pompeii (Electa)

Amedeo Maiuri (15th Edition)
Pompeii (Istituto Poligrafico Dello Stato)

Michael Grant (2001)
*Cities of Vesuvius. Pompeii and
Herculaneum* (Phoenix Press)

Joseph Jay Deiss (1995)
*The Town of Hercules: A Buried Treasure
Trove* (The J. Paul Getty Museum)

Seneca
Naturales Questiones vols VII and X,
Trans. T. H. Corcoran. Harvard University
Press, Cambridge, Mass, 1971. Reprinted
by Loeb Classical Library.

Pliny
Letters of the Younger Pliny, Trans. B.
Radice 1963. Penguin Classics 1969

Goethe
Italian Journey, Trans. W. H. Auden,
1962. Harper Collins Publishers Ltd.

Livy
The History of Rome, Trans. Evan T. Sage.
Loeb Classical Library, Harvard University
Press.

Tacitus
Annals and Dialogus de Oratoribus,
Trans. John Jackson.

Juvenal
The Sixteen Satires, Trans. P. Green,
Penguin 1967.

Martial
Epigrams, 1969, Loeb Classical Library,
Harvard University Press.

Charles Dickens
Pictures from Italy, 1846

Mark Twain
The Innocents Abroad, 1875

Guido Piovene
Travels in Italy, 1958

Vitruvius
Ten Books of Architecture,
Trans. Morris Hicky Morgan. New York,
Dover publications 1960

INDEX